W9-CZU-783

ℬ

# SPIRITUAL LEADERSHIP FOR CHALLENGING TIMES

## Presidential Addresses from the Leadership Conference of Women Religious

Edited by
Annmarie Sanders, IHM

ORBIS  BOOKS

Maryknoll, New York 10545

ORBIS BOOKS
Maryknoll, New York 10545

Fathers and Brothers
MARYKNOLL™

Founded in 1970, Orbis Books endeavors to publish works that enlighten the mind, nourish the spirit, and challenge the conscience. The publishing arm of the Maryknoll Fathers and Brothers, Orbis seeks to explore the global dimensions of the Christian faith and mission, to invite dialogue with diverse cultures and religious traditions, and to serve the cause of reconciliation and peace. The books published reflect the views of their authors and do not represent the official position of the Maryknoll Society. To learn more about Maryknoll and Orbis Books, please visit our website at www.maryknollsociety.org.

Copyright © 2014 by the Leadership Conference of Women Religious.

Published by Orbis Books, Box 302, Maryknoll, NY 10545-0302.

All rights reserved.

No part of this publication may be reproduced or transmitted in any form or by any means, electronic or mechanical, including photocopying, recording, or any information storage or retrieval system, without prior permission in writing from the publisher.

Queries regarding rights and permissions should be addressed to: Orbis Books, P.O. Box 302, Maryknoll, NY 10545-0302.

Manufactured in the United States of America

Library of Congress Cataloging-in-Publication Data
Spiritual leadership for challenging times : presidential addresses from the
Leadership Conference of Women Religious / Annmarie Sanders, IHM, editor.
    pages     cm
    ISBN 978-1-62698-066-2 (pbk.)
    1. Monasticism and religious orders for women—United States—
Congresses. 2. Women in church work—Catholic Church—Congresses.
3. Christian leadership—Congresses. 4. Leadership—Religious aspects—
Catholic Church—Congresses. 5. Leadership Conference of Women
Religious of the United States.  I. Sanders, Annmarie, editor of compilation.
II. Leadership Conference of Women Religious of the United States.
BX4220.U6S68 2014
271'.90073—dc23                                        2013030456

# SPIRITUAL LEADERSHIP
# FOR CHALLENGING TIMES

# CONTENTS

# ACKNOWLEDGMENTS

The Leadership Conference of Women Religious offers its deep gratitude to all who made this collection of addresses possible.

We thank first the forty-eight women who have generously served in the presidency of this conference of leaders since its founding in 1956. The organization has faced numerous challenges throughout the years and these women consistently provided extraordinary leadership, while at the same time administering their own institutes of women religious. These speeches and reports of all these LCWR presidents demonstrate the exercise of strong spiritual leadership in complex times. Selecting only ten of these addresses for this collection was a difficult task.

We are grateful for the committee that studied each presidential address and selected those that seemed most appropriate for this volume. These women — Sister Helen Maher Garvey, BVM; Sister Sheila Lemieux, CSJP; Mary J. Novak; Sister Rita Parks, RSM; Sister Annmarie Sanders, IHM; and Sister Marlene Weisenbeck, FSPA — gave most generously of their time and expertise. Special thanks go to Sister Helen for writing the introduction to this volume and to Sister Rita for creating an introduction to each address that notes the significant world and ecclesial events of that time. We thank as well LCWR's executive director, Sister Janet Mock, CSJ who not only supported the production of this book, but also authored its epilogue.

When LCWR looked for assistance with clerical tasks in preparing these addresses, several women stepped forward as generous volunteers: Sister Elaine Frank, OSF; Sister Vivien Linkhauer, SC; Sister Thea O'Meara, BVM, Sister Patty Morriset, OP; Sister Marianne Raumussen, OSF; Sister Theresa Sandok, OMU; and Amy Strickland. We are grateful as well to LCWR staff member Chris Costello for her careful reading of the manuscript.

Finally, we thank Sister Sandra Schneiders, IHM, who first planted in us the seed of an idea for this book, recognizing the hunger that exists in the world for spiritual leadership; and Robert Ellsberg, publisher at Orbis Books and the editor of this volume, whose wise advice and generous assistance have been invaluable.

# PREFACE

For many American Catholics, their first awareness of the Leadership Conference of Women Religious (LCWR) came on April 18, 2012, with the release to the public of the findings of the doctrinal assessment of the organization by the Congregation for the Doctrine of the Faith (CDF).

The doctrinal assessment, which the CDF initiated in 2008, noted that the doctrinal and pastoral situation of the LCWR, an organization that serves the leaders of congregations of Catholic sisters in the United States, was "grave and a matter of serious concern." It declared that the LCWR's assemblies, speakers, publications, and programs provided evidence of "problematic statements and serious theological, even doctrinal errors" as well as the prevalence of "radical feminist themes."

With the approval of Pope Benedict XVI, the CDF executed a mandate (detailed in the April 18, 2012, document) to assist in "the necessary reform" of the LCWR through the appointment of an archbishop delegate who would work with a group of advisors to address the problems outlined in the assessment findings.

The LCWR, however, found the assessment process itself flawed and the findings based on unsubstantiated accusations. In a public statement issued on June 1, 2012, it also noted that the sanctions outlined in the mandate were "disproportionate to the concerns raised" and compromised the organization's ability to fulfill its mission.

In the months that followed the release of the CDF document, the situation between the CDF and the LCWR drew attention from the media worldwide. As a result, the LCWR experienced an outpouring of communications. While some people expressed support for the CDF assessment, the vast majority noted their interest in and desire for the type of leadership provided by the LCWR and by Catholic sisters in general in various ecclesial and professional settings throughout the country and world. Nearly a hundred thousand Catholics and persons of other faiths expressed through letters, e-mails, petitions, and phone calls, as well as through prayer vigils around the country, a profound resonance with the vision, mission, and works of the LCWR. Over and over people declared their hunger for a strong spiritual leadership for both the world and church that was keenly attuned to the signs of the times and willing to adapt to new knowledge and insights.

The media also closely followed the LCWR's annual Assembly held that year in St. Louis in August. The gathering of approximately nine hundred Catholic sister leaders was the first opportunity for the membership of the organization to discuss the implications of the CDF findings and mandate and to reflect together on how to respond. After much discussion and prayerful discernment, the strong consensus of the members at the close of the Assembly was to charge its officers to enter into a conversation with the archbishop delegate appointed to oversee the reform of the LCWR, with the hope that open and honest dialogue would lead not only to increasing understanding between the church leadership and women religious, but also to "creating more possibilities for the laity and, particularly for women, to have a voice in the church."

While that process of dialogue continues, the interest on the part of the public in the work of the LCWR and the type of reconciling, dialogic leadership it has historically sought to foster and strengthen in its members grows. In part to respond to that interest in spiritual leadership for these complex times, the LCWR has compiled this collection of presidential addresses from the past thirty-five years. The hope is that readers will find ideas and inspiration as they formulate their own understandings of the type of leadership that is needed in the world and church today as together we work to meet the needs of all people as well as prepare for a sustainable future for generations to come.

ANNMARIE SANDERS, IHM
Director of Communications
Leadership Conference
of Women Religious

# INTRODUCTION

Waves of thunderous applause resounded through the grand ball-room of the Millennium Hotel in St. Louis on August 10, 2012. Pro-longing the standing ovation, many participants in the Assembly of the Leadership Conference of Women Religious (LCWR) wept. In the midst of this tumult stood the speaker, a native of Waterloo, Iowa, a member of the Sisters of St. Francis of Dubuque, Iowa, a reserved missionary, the president of the LCWR, Pat Farrell, OSF. She came to this moment reluctantly as the Conference and many lay supporters struggled to understand the doctrinal assessment of the LCWR released just months earlier by the Vatican's Congrega-tion for the Doctrine of the Faith (CDF).[1] Previously, the LCWR board had described the Vatican's procedure as the "result of a flawed process that lacked transparency."

Capturing the spirit of the Assembly, Farrell's address concluded with the expression "They can crush a few flowers but they can't hold back the springtime." These words and this address, a compelling call for dialogue and integrity, would reverberate in press releases, media appearances (including 60 Minutes), and public presentations by the organization's leaders. So who is this organization? Whence comes this passion? Why such national interest?

In November 1956, after several preliminary meetings, 235 major superiors of American communities of Catholic sisters gath-ered in Chicago. Responding to the request of Vatican authorities, they considered the formation of a national conference of the supe-riors of women's religious congregations. Many in the gathering were not enthusiastic about doing so, but just before taking the vote, one of the superiors present announced to the group "Rome wishes it." The Conference of Major Superiors of Women (CMSW) came into being with 90 percent of the superiors of women's communities in the United States as members.[2]

Just a few short years later, the Catholic Church experienced the most significant religious event in the twentieth century, the Second Vatican Council. For women religious the council exploded in the thunderclap of two documents: *Perfectae Caritatis* (1965), Decree on the Renewal and Adaptation of Religious Life, and *Gaudium et Spes* (1965), Pastoral Constitution on the Church in the Modern World. *Perfectae Caritatis* called them to renew their lives in the light of the Gospel, the signs of the times, and the charisms of their congregations. *Gaudium et Spes* sounded a keynote for mission: "The joys and the hopes, the griefs and the anxieties of the men of this age, especially those who are poor or in any way afflicted, these are the joys and hopes, the griefs and anxieties of the followers of Christ."[3] The spirit of these documents would forever reverberate in the life of the Conference.

While responding to the spirit of Vatican II, the Conference accomplished the ordinary tasks of forming an organization, drafting constitutions, bylaws, regional boundaries, membership policies. By the late sixties and early seventies, however, internal conflict erupted among members with different ecclesiologies. This clash reached a critical point during the 1971 meeting in Atlanta when the organization changed its name to the Leadership Conference of Women Religious.

A splinter group of members formed a new organization, *Consortium Perfectae Caritatis* (CPC). This group drew members concerned that the newly named LCWR was deviating from "authentic" church teaching about the essentials of religious life. Although the LCWR initiated many efforts to heal this breach, the rupture deepened, and in 1992 the Vatican approved a second leadership conference of women religious in the United States, the Council of Major Superiors of Women Religious (CMSWR).

While addressing this challenge, the LCWR continued its mission of "assisting its members personally and communally to carry out more collaboratively their service of leadership in order to accomplish further the mission of Christ in today's world." Throughout the years, the themes of *Perfectae Caritatis* and *Gaudium et Spes* animated the Conference. A fierce commitment to the spirit of Vatican II galvanized its very life and promoted an evolution of themes and commitments. *Perfectae Caritatis's* call to the Gospel, the original charism, and the signs of the times provided its essential vision. *Gaudium et Spes*, with its "joys and hopes," enlivened the mission with the poetry of the poor. The church is for the world. The Conference is for the world.

The riches of the Conference, its evolution, even its struggles and failures do not belong to the Conference alone. Just as the Conference has learned from its members, from the church, from its interfaith relationships, and from society, so too it owes the fruits of its life to others. Through this book the LCWR offers a selection of its presidential addresses. It was difficult to make choices among the many outstanding examples considered. Many other addresses could have been included in this collection. Though excellent, some presentations did not fit the focus of this project. It was the overriding theme of this collection—the spirituality of leadership—that ultimately helped to determine its content.

It is this spirituality of leadership that the LCWR proposes to its readers. Originating within a group of hierarchical leaders in a hierarchical church, these Catholic sisters evolved and are evolving their leadership into a process of inclusion, contemplation, and decision. Vision and mission driven, this leadership encourages the art of listening, sharing, disagreeing, searching, praying, navigating the tension between consensus and prophecy, and finding common ground. It assumes relationships in a living organism, a web of relationships, beginning with conversation, fostering collaboration, and evoking communion. It sometimes causes pain and tension, probing both the minds and hearts of the participants. This spiritual leadership reaches deep into the contemplative soul of the organization and reflects that soul.

This contemplative soul, this vision of spiritual leadership, finds expression in the LCWR's *Dimensions of Leadership*,[4] which calls leaders to articulate deep rootedness in God, connect the soul of the organization with the soul of the global church and the soul of the world, and articulate a dynamic sense of the charism.

Living this ideal in our turbulent times recalls Abraham Lincoln's counsel.

> Still the question recurs, "Can we do better?" The dogmas
> of the quiet past are inadequate to the stormy present. The
> occasion is piled high with difficulty, and we must rise with
> the occasion. As our case is new, so we must think anew and
> act anew.[5]

Presidents and the members of the Conference have often thought
anew and acted anew. Scanning the vocabulary of the Conference's
addresses over the years provides a glimpse into the heart of women
religious in contemporary times and their concerns: justice, spirituality of leadership, identity, service, dialogue, contemplation, relationships, women, prophecy, solidarity with the marginalized, impasse,
globalization, discernment, hope, nonviolence, conscience. A clear
focus on the signs of the times emerges: civil rights, ecology, human
trafficking, war, evolving consciousness, terrorism, immigration, the
dignity of women.

Response to these signs of the times emerges from the charism of
religious life. What is this charism? Charism means that religious life
is directly dependent upon the Spirit, both in its origins and in its
continually new forms. The charism of religious life is the fruit of the
Holy Spirit who is always at work within the church.[6]

Fidelity to the charism, the founding spirit, is often troublesome.
*Mutuae Relationes* tells us that "every authentic charism implies a
certain element of genuine originality and of special initiative for
the spiritual life of the church. In its surroundings, it may appear
troublesome and may even cause difficulties, since it is not always
and immediately easy to recognize it as coming from the Spirit."[7]

Striving to articulate the genuine originality of the charism
of the LCWR, presidential addresses evidence a whole spectrum
of realities: challenge, conflict, joy, frustration, uncertainty, hope,
and prophetic truth. Celebrating this charism, the LCWR in 2009
mounted an exhibition, *Women & Spirit: Catholic Sisters in America*.
Viewed by more than one million persons in venues throughout the
United States, its purpose was to document the significant leadership
role of Catholic sisters in social change, in building the social fabric

of the country through education, health care, and social service. It recalled the story of the contribution of untold women religious to the nation beginning with the arrival of the Ursuline Sisters in New Orleans in 1727.

Simultaneously, the LCWR, in collaboration with Design Island, produced a companion documentary, *Women & Spirit,* narrated by the noted author and senior news analyst Cokie Roberts. It features interviews with historians, journalists, and sisters, and brings to life the inspiring story, both personal and communal, of women who have greatly helped to shape the American landscape.

In that landscape and internationally, the LCWR continues to support a spirited dialogue among LCWR leaders, and members, communities, and with church and society. It brings to that conversation the fruits of its life of renewal: a strong sense of the dignity of women, solidarity with the poor, commitment to discernment, integrity in conflict, a fierce sense of justice, and a budding evolution of consciousness. In this endeavor the LCWR reveals a spirituality of leadership. Here, in these pages, you will find this spirituality of leadership woven through the themes of the presidential addresses. Here, in these pages, you will discover the life, the heritage, and the vision of the Leadership Conference of Women Religious.

HELEN MAHER Garvey, BVM

## Notes

1. The Apostolic Constitution on the Roman Curia, *Pastor Bonus,* promulgated by John Paul II on June 28, 1988, states: "The duty proper to the Congregation for the Doctrine of the Faith is to promote and safeguard the doctrine on the faith and morals throughout the Catholic world."

2. Lora Ann Quiñonez, CDP, and Mary Daniel Turner, SNDdeN, *Transformation of American Catholic Sisters* (Philadelphia: Temple University Press, 1992).

3. *Gaudium et Spes,* Pastoral Constitution on the Church in the Modern World, Second Vatican Council, December 7, 1965, 1.

4. Leadership Conference of Women Religious of the United States, *Dimensions of Skills and Competencies for Effective Leadership* (Silver Spring, MD: LCWR, 1997).

5. Abraham Lincoln, Second Annual Message to Congress, December 1, 1862.

6. Paul VI, *Evangelica Testificatio*, On the Renewal of the Religious Life according to the Teaching of the Second Vatican Council, June 29, 1971, 11.

7. Sacred Congregation for Religious and for Secular Institutes, Sacred Congregation for Bishops, *Mutuae Relationes*, Directives for the Mutual Relations between Bishops and Religious in the Church, May 14, 1978, 12.

# 1

*1977 National Assembly*
*"It Is a Journey"*

## MAKING THE FUTURE POSSIBLE

### *Joan Chittister, OSB*

— Chicago, August 28, 1977 —

*Naming is an attempt to describe reality, to confer upon that reality a persona and a purpose. The 1971 Conference decision to shift the language of its descriptive title from "Major Superiors" to "Women Religious" and to add "Leadership" signaled a changed reality. The years between 1971 and the annual August LCWR Assembly in 1977, when Joan Chittister addressed the members as their president, were years of further changes.*

*Those years witnessed a world drained after decades of conflict in Vietnam, yet harboring faint hopes for peace in the Middle East. In the Southern Hemisphere, African colonialism and apartheid felt the pressure for change, while Latin American citizens vanished or suffered rape, torture, and imprisonment under dictatorial regimes. Terrorism stalked the Berlin Olympics on the ground and international flights in the skies. In the United States, the Pentagon Papers revealed that the government had long misled the American people about the war in Southeast Asia, while the Watergate scandal led to the resignation of a president. The Supreme Court ruled on abortion in Roe v. Wade and ordered busing to integrate schools. Meanwhile, debate raged on euthanasia and the right to die. Star Wars opened almost simultaneously with the creation of Apple and Microsoft, and the 1975 celebration of International Women's Year saw once again the failure of enough states to ratify the Equal Rights Amendment to the U.S. Constitution.*

*Churches offered sanctuary to refugees fleeing the conflicts in Central America; parishioners welcomed people who fled by boat from Vietnam and Cambodia; women and men religious and clergy joined farm workers in civil disobedience. Pope Paul VI promoted world evangelization; the Vatican defended infallibility and banned women priests, while the Episcopal Church moved to ordain them. Large numbers of religious departed from convents and monasteries while a committee of the U.S. bishops called for a study of women in church ministry. The Consortium Perfectae Caritatis sought approval as an alternative conference to the LCWR, and the LCWR was granted nongovernmental status at the United Nations.*

*Within this milieu, and "under the siege of new needs in church and society," this presidential address reflected a challenge for women in leadership to "go deeper but differently into life, into service, into God."*

This year's Assembly, Sisters, presents a terrible temptation for someone who is first on a program. The temptation is to drift into metaphor and to be poetic. The call, if this is a call, is not intended to be that. It is intended to be what is, from my point of view, an honest analysis of the present alternatives in religious life. The Assembly that we are opening tonight is a public admission of unfinishedness called "Journey." It is also therefore a public proclamation of a continuing commitment to grow. The Benedictines call it "to seek God who ever calls anew." In 1968 we, the women in this room, most of us, began together to call ourselves to rigorous self-assessment. This was a beginning. Tonight in utter seriousness we call ourselves not only to consider where we are—we have done so much of that—but to begin to proclaim together and publicly where women religious, after ten years of search, are beginning to feel that religious life must go. The presentation I make tonight is meant to be backdrop to that effort. Before we begin the week, then, I submit for your consideration three items: what I consider to be a model of religious life, a description of its current situation, and an analysis of the challenges which I personally believe confront those of us who are in leadership positions in religious communities today.

The model is a motley one. It is from the second book of Kings, chapter 7. It is a very simple but a graphic story, and you probably remember it well. Jerusalem, the writer says, is suffering siege and the situation is very extreme. The city has been surrounded for so long that within the walls they lack, for the first time in their conscious history, both water and food, the very staples of life.

The bony heads of asses are being sold for eighty shekels and are the supper of nobles. The women of the poor have even begun to plot plans to identify which of their children will be eaten first. And, outside, the enemy makes no move to attack. There is no reason to attack. They can simply wait for the Israelites within the city to die, because Israel has lost its inner resources, its energy, and its will to confront its real problems. Instead they go on day after day business as usual and wait for Yahweh to save them. These Israelites in this city apparently don't notice or at least they certainly don't care about four lepers who in this period sit at the city gates. But the lepers, weakened though they are, marginal and outcast—never such a healthy lot, come to think about it—are facing the situation and considering what they might do. One leper says, "Well, it is useless to go back into the city, because if we go back into the city, we shall surely die." And the second leper says, "Well, it is useless to stay here by the city gates; what is to be gained by this, by simply waiting?" The third one says, "Then there is only one thing to do and that is to go into the Amorite camp itself, because there, you see, we have a fifty–fifty chance. Either we will be accepted and saved, or we shall die—the last lot no worse than this one." It's a very serious decision for any Israelite to make. They must decide to leave the old city, the Chosen People. They must decide to go to new territory; they must decide to yield apparently to pagan influences. The writer tells us, "The lepers went in *darkness*."

But a marvelous thing happens. Yahweh goes before the lepers with the sound of great din, so loud that the attacking enemy believes that somehow or other the Israelites must have been able to hire mercenaries who are coming down upon them, and so they flee the camp, leaving the tents full and the table set. By the time the lepers get to the new territory, to what they thought would be the camp of the enemy, they find full tents, an empty camp and, like you tonight, gifts in the wilderness. Then, realizing their responsibilities, they say, "It is not right for us to stay here; our responsibility is to return to the city." In that way the whole community of Israel is liberated, renewed, and made effective in the world again.

This siege and these lepers, I believe, are a model of the present development and, as a matter of fact, the traditional development of religious life. Five times in history religious life has been under siege. It has been under the siege of new needs in church and society. Each time the response to the siege has been a drastic change in the image, in the basic mode of living religious life so that the religious who followed could go deeper but differently into life, into service, into God. The desert fathers, for instance—the prototype religious—became solitary ascetics in their society so that they could witness to and maintain a spirit of total commitment in a society where Christianity had become a state religion, where state religions were civic norms and most of the time, therefore, no religion at all. The desert fathers were the model of religious life from the second to the fifth century, but then there were new needs in church and society.

When the order of the Roman Empire collapsed, the monks joined together and formed stable communities, not as solitary hermits in the desert, but as groups of committed people living together who became the life centers of Western Europe from the fifth to the twelfth century. But in the beginning of this new response of religious life they were called lax. Clearly our founder, St. Benedict, was aware of this criticism. Three places in the Rule he points out that we will not be living like those who have gone before us. We lax monks, he says, won't be doing all those things. It took the Benedictines two hundred years to be accepted in the church.

In the thirteenth century a new set of world forces shaped the world state. Cities rose, nationalism raged, and mendicant communities developed. These communities said, in essence, stability was fine—Benedictines, when everybody was on the farm—but it won't work now. Mobility is what is being asked of those who serve the Christ in the kingdom of God. And the mendicants emerged to follow the poor, to serve the poor, to be with the poor. The words of St. Francis record: "I know they will try to make you monastics but don't let them. I am another kind of fool."

At a fourth point in history, when the political power and unity of the church declined, the apostolic orders rose to defend the church, the papacy, and the dogma and make spiritual cohesion the overriding service of religious orders until the eighteenth century. But for these people, in order to serve the church and the people of God as it needed to be served in that period, founder after founder of the communities in this room had to tell their followers do not call yourself religious, or the church will not let you serve the way we must.

At the fifth point in the cycle, in the nineteenth century, as a period of enlightenment and democracy emerged, teaching congregations rose to do radical things which brought fire to the city of Philadelphia and criticism to the church. Teaching congregations were radical and bold enough to empower the masses, to liberate the poor.

Each of these major images of religious life emerged out of changes: changes in the church, changes in society. Each one of those images diminished the image before it. Each one of those images was met with official hostility. The world and the church are changing again, changing even now as we set out in this week to begin to articulate a theology of religious life. The church's definition of itself, the world problematic, and a new notion of woman are forming the base of a new worldview. What conclusions can we draw at beginning this week?

- ◆ First, major social or ecclesial changes create new needs.

- ◆ Second, new needs bring changes in the nature—the very nature—of religious life.

- Third, in the past only those communities survived who were capable of new modes of response. Sixty-six percent of all the religious communities founded before the year 1800 are now extinct.

- Fourth, religious life, I would submit, is at the gates of the city again, in transition to a new era. Like the lepers, there are before us three possibilities. We can go back into the city; we can stay where we are—it's getting comfortable; or we can risk moving toward a new vision of religious life—provided we are willing to move in darkness and in uncertainty. For the new vision—like many before it—is in tension with the old.

The old vision of religious life says that the purpose of religious life is to be a labor force, to do institutional work. There is a new vision rising that says no. The purpose of religious life is to be a leaven in society, to be a caring presence, to be nomads who go first where others cannot go.

The old vision of religious life says that religious take vows to keep laws, but a new vision is emerging which signals now that religious take vows to gain life and to give life.

The old vision says that the vow enables us to show what we are against: that we are against too many things, too dangerous a relationship, too much self. The new vision of religious life says that the purpose of vows is to be for something: to be for the poor, to be for love and justice, to be for the responsible use of talents, to be for a dynamic relationship with Christ. The new vision of the vows says that vows are creative, not negative.

The old vision of religious life says that religious life is a state of perfection, and that therefore we must be very careful; we must be very correct; we must be very approved. What will the lay people say? The new vision of religious life says that religious life is a search, that it is one state of Christian growth as defined in *Lumen Gentium*, that it is a sign that Gospel is possible, joyful, and other-centered.

The old vision of religious life says that the purpose of religious is to transcend the world, to withdraw, to be private, to be quiet. The new vision of religious life says that the purpose of a religious is to transform the world, like the Christ before it. To be in it but not of it.

So to be a religious leader in a period of transition or siege is to have to make a leper's choice. To face new questions with only old answers as a guide. And though there are many issues we could talk about tonight, Sisters—ministry, retirement, community, membership, maintenance—there is only one central challenge, I believe, and that is the challenge of leadership itself. Women who sit in this room tonight have an awesome and immediate responsibility for the future and the very survival of their congregations.

I present for your consideration four circumstances which constitute the crises and challenges confronting administrators of religious communities today, as I see them.

One. We must realize that renewal is not over. In fact it may barely have begun. Leaders of the early period of renewal indeed were great strong women who faced resistance, a high level of emotion, a lot of struggle, a great deal of shock, and much criticism. But those women also had high hopes rising across this country, had a period of great energy, were supported in their position by a sense of expectation. New leaders—leaders in office tonight, leaders recently elected, leaders who will be chosen six months from now—face the heat of the day. They face the fatigue that goes with long, slow efforts. They are tired, their sisters are tired, the parish is tired, the bishop is tired. The people are tired, hot, discouraged, tempted to wonder sometimes if beginning was worth it. The point I'm trying to make is that, in its own way—given a trend or a movement in history, given a time and a call and a tide—beginnings are relatively easy. It is going on that's hard—not settling down—not turning back; not giving up takes courage and leadership. I ask you to remember this week as you make difficult statements that Moses indeed led the Chosen People out of Egypt, but Joshua led them into the Promised Land. If the leaders who follow the leaders who began stop, then it's over. Religious communities do not need and perhaps will not be able to survive as caretakers for Chosen People. We need leaders who have a capacity for wilderness and the longest, darkest part of the trip.

Two. I believe that we must realize that to be aware itself is to be sent. That is a sign of the sending. I am saying that consciousness is of the essence of prophecy. The realization of the message is what really commissioned every prophet. None of the prophets I know were called and told, "Be here at the mountain at three tomorrow afternoon and I'm going to give you a message." They got the message whether they wanted it or not and were told to start. Every prophet—Moses, Jonah, Amos—none of them wanted to criticize the king. All of them argued that they couldn't do it. Others, ones who went before, they said, were better equipped. They all argued that the people would be upset. Paul, too. Romans, chapters nine and ten, the most poignant passage of any of his epistles, I think, is full of misery. Paul said, "What happened to the covenant we loved? Where did it go and why did it go?" He loved the Old Covenant and he loved the Israelites who were clinging to it and he knew that some of them would go on clinging, Christ or not. But his new understandings, his new call, and his new vision pressed him beyond it, even though in the scripture he describes himself as having "great grief and constant pain."

Three. I think we must accept the fact that the purpose of leadership is not to make the present bearable. The purpose of leadership is to make the future possible. We must remember then that many things for which we strive may never be gained in our lifetime. But our debt is not to yesterday. Our debt is not even to today. Our debt is to those who come tomorrow, that they can come in dignity and faith. So as we watch one hope and one goal after another be continually unrealized, we must learn to gather strength for the distance ahead from the notion that what may not be for us can be because of us.

Finally, like the Israelites under siege, we cannot now afford to succumb to pressures, to succumb faithlessly in fear. We cannot succumb to the inwardness of our communities. We cannot become reluctant leaders. Reluctant leadership is worse than no leadership at all. Do not state something and then wring your hands for fear it will happen. Of all the religious in this country we are the ones who must go into the wilderness. No, we must lead into a wilderness that is once again taking us deeper and differently into life, into service, into God. We have an obligation, Sisters, to everyone in the city, to pursue the new vision with the same kind of commitment, courage, personal discipline, and rigorous sacrifice with which we pursued the last. We too have an obligation to go beyond the city gates—to go indeed where there is no trail and leave a path.

# 2

*1980 National Assembly*
*"Once upon a Conviction"*

# TO SPEAK THE TRUTH IN LOVE

## *M. Theresa Kane, RSM*

— Philadelphia, August 24, 1980 —

*If the address of 1977 issued a challenge to pursue a new vision with commitment and courage, the short span between 1977 and August 1980 provided ample opportunity for a spirited response.*

A newly elected John Paul II visited the United States, and Theresa Kane as LCWR president welcomed him and urged full participation for women in the ministries of the church. Meanwhile, Archbishop Oscar Romero was murdered in El Salvador, and Cuban refugees boarded makeshift boats heading for Florida. Soviet troops were entering Afghanistan, Sandinista rebels had overcome the ruling Nicaraguan Somoza dynasty, and Iran was now an Islamic republic. The Three Mile Island nuclear plant in Pennsylvania experienced a partial meltdown, while the SALT II treaty moved to limit missile launching facilities. The same year that mass suicides in Jonestown, Guyana, destroyed families, the first test-tube baby was born. Iranians took hostages at the embassy in Tehran, Ronald Reagan succeeded Jimmy Carter as U.S. president, and Saddam Hussein became president of Iraq. A fundamentalist televangelist initiated the Moral Majority in the United States a few short months before a trade union organizer cofounded Solidarity in Poland. In outer space, Soviet cosmonauts set a record for earth orbiting, and the U.S. Voyager snapped photos of Jupiter's moons.

With events tumbling rapidly one upon another worldwide, nationally, and locally, this address—centered as it is on speaking the truth to *oneself, to the other, and to church and society—added a sharp focus on women in these arenas as the LCWR began its celebration of twenty-five years of leadership and service to its members.*

It is a distinct privilege to come before you this evening as one who has strived to serve this Conference during the past year as president, as sister, as friend. It is an honor to formally open the 1980 LCWR Assembly. The theme chosen by the program committee—"Once upon a Conviction"—can be challenging, inspiring, and provocative if we enter fully into the Assembly story during these next few days.

The title I have given my talk this evening is "To Speak the Truth in Love." For a moment let us reflect on the words recorded in Ephesians 4:

> Let us profess the truth in love and grow
> to the full maturity of Christ the head.

Let us attempt to discern what this message can mean for the women of the Leadership Conference of Women Religious as we continue to journey, not only in an identity as women religious, but in an identity as women, as persons. In reflecting upon this theme "To Speak the Truth in Love" I have identified four aspects:

- to speak the truth in love to oneself;

- to speak the truth in love to each other;

- to speak the truth in love to the institutional church; and finally,

- and finally to speak the truth in love to the institutional society.

In addition, I would like to highlight three concerns to which we as leaders in our congregations and as members of the LCWR need to direct our attention during the coming days and into the coming years. These are the specific concerns I wish to highlight:

- the "return to prayer" syndrome;

- the need to rejuvenate the missionary spirit of our apostolic services; and

- the need to denounce war as a form of institutional violence.

The program calls this address the "keynote address." I do not wish to be perceived as a "keynoter." I desire to share honestly and respectfully the fruits of my reflections as I complete this year as president. In a spirit of reverence, charity, and interior freedom I present my hopes, concerns, and visions as they may affect this Conference. Throughout the coming days I welcome your reflections on anything I say this evening. It is only in such a dialogic atmosphere that we can strive to minimize a spirit of fear and domination, even with and among ourselves. During this past year a statement has been made to me by several members of the hierarchy: "There are issues in the church that are not open to dialogue." That statement itself causes paralysis and fear and needs to be challenged whenever it is heard.

## To Speak the Truth in Love to Oneself

Such a stance requires honesty and courage but most of all a certain measure of confidence in oneself, and confidence in the Spirit who directs the promptings of one's heart. Women, particularly, need to listen to the stirrings which are welling within them. For all too long women have followed laws and directions which have been truly "man-made." Persons engaged in feminist theology and spirituality believe that women need to internalize and articulate a feminist spirituality that is latent within them. Traditionally, with few exceptions, the church recognized only men as teachers, as doctors, and as spiritual directors. As women we have a serious responsibility to articulate a feminist theology of religious life. To do so, we must be in contact with our own feelings, experiences, and reflections. One result of speaking truth within oneself in relation to a new spirituality will be a revolutionary approach to God. A sense of intuition that becomes conscious of its femininity will challenge the ancient concept of God as Father, as male, and as a Being always portrayed as one sex to the total exclusion of the other sex. Such a distorted image of God must be eliminated if a feminist spirituality of God is to develop among both men and women.

To speak the truth in love to oneself is essential before one's truth is shared with others. To begin with self—striving always to root out the sinful elements of disintegration within one's person. This is a first challenge. Paradoxically, because women have been almost totally outside of church and society as systems, there is a corresponding freedom that enables women to speak truth. Such truth cannot fall on deaf ears.

## To Speak the Truth in Love to Each Other

Women religious have been engaged in a revolutionary process of transforming religious life as an institution since even before the advent of Vatican Council II. However, the council accelerated and intensified the renewal efforts for women religious so that as we approach the decade of the 1980s, we do so with a renewed sense of identity and maturity. It must be considered revolution when one reflects that a complete "turning around" of so many facets of the institution known as religious life have been affected. We have critically evaluated and renewed areas of religious dress, governance models, lifestyles, and ministries. Now we are engaging in serious dialogue with the women in our congregations, and with each other, about the constitutions which articulate the revolution which has taken place. How urgent it is that we speak truth in love to each other about the process, engaging the members of our congregations in developing the documents which articulate and express our lives. At the present time a sense of anxiety, perhaps even fear, seems to cloud some congregations of women because of what is perceived as a canonical deadline for having constitutions approved. We must speak truthfully to each other about our experiences, both positive and negative, as we formally submit constitutions to Rome. When considering our relationship with the institutional church as it is reflected in either approval or disapproval of the constitutions, one cannot but ask: "Are the systems of the institutional church such that a close scrutiny of details affecting women's congregations might be another example of paternalism?" Perhaps constitutions should not be subject to minute scrutiny at any time and certainly not at a time when they have not yet been sufficiently tested by the women who have articulated them. Perhaps we should be speaking with each other about whether or not the present church structures for approval of congregational constitutions are either necessary or helpful to the life and ministries of the respective religious congregations. Should another structure replace the present Sacred Congregation for Religious and Secular Institutes (SCRIS)? How do women whose lives are directly affected by the SCRIS structure have any influence on its reform or effect a transformation of its structures that more justly express a new religious life? Perhaps a structure such as a peer review panel might be initiated by the LCWR for its members. Such a panel could review and critique documents for those who desire it. Also, when a congregation of women religious does complete its constitutions, it has a responsibility to engage the structures of SCRIS in a serious dialogue with the religious community. Canonical approval of constitutions would then neither be requested nor granted; such an ongoing dialogic posture between religious communities of women and the SCRIS structure would reflect a relationship of maturity, mutuality, and equality.

## To Speak the Truth In Love
## to the Institutional Church

Perhaps the example of constitutions exemplifies how necessary it is for women to dialogue about such matters among themselves. It also illustrates how women need to speak the truth in love to the institutional church. In 1971, the Synod of Bishops issued a powerful challenge to the entire church community in its document *Justice in the World*. Women religious received this challenge, and it became a primary document circulated among women in the decade of the 1970s. The entire document is indeed worthy of serious review, but in addressing myself to the question of speaking the truth to the institutional church, I quote from one section of the document:

> While the Church is bound to give witness to justice, she recognizes that anyone who ventures to speak to people about justice must first be just in their eyes.

The above passage is a critical one when we reflect upon our responsibility and obligation to speak truth in love to our church. The Roman Catholic Church as an institution must recognize and acknowledge the serious social injustices which by its very system are imposed upon women of the Roman Catholic Church. The church, in its documents, affirms the dignity, reverence, and equality of all persons. The institutional church preaches this message to the peoples and governments of our world. Until the institutional Catholic Church undertakes a serious, critical examination of its mode of acting toward women, it cannot, it will not give witness to justice in the world. The challenge for women in the 1980s is to confront and eradicate the systemic evils of sexism, clericalism, and paternalism. The Roman Catholic Church is a divine institution whose strength comes from the promise of Jesus: "I am with you always, until the end of the world!" This promise of Jesus does not negate the fact that the church is also a human institution and, therefore, subject to the social evils of other human systems. For two thousand years women have been systemically excluded from the church as institution. The Roman Catholic Church cannot profess dignity, reverence, and equality for all persons and continue to systemically exclude women as persons from fully participating in the institutional church. In addition to being excluded from the institutional church, women have at times been victims of the church's structure. I want to take this moment to illustrate with a few stories how the LCWR particularly has been a victim of the institutional church's sexism and paternalism.

This summer the past presidents of the Leadership Conference of Women Religious gathered together for a few days in an attempt to share the oral history of the Conference. It was a renewing experience, and I was inspired by the commitment and dedication of the women present. I cite from among many experiences the following three examples, which led us to conclude at the end of the past presidents' conference that although as a Leadership Conference we had achieved a sense of mutual understanding and dialogue with individual members of the hierarchy, we had to admit sadly that no systemic change toward women within the institutional church was evident to us:

1.  Sister Betty Carroll, serving as president in 1971–72 and then known as Sister Thomas Aquinas Carroll, was truly a victim of unfortunate circumstances because of an opinion regarding religious dress circulated directly to the U.S. hierarchy and not to either the women's communities, to the LCWR, nor to the president of the LCWR. Representatives of SCRIS determined that it was opportune to issue an "opinion" on the question of religious dress. At the time a number of congregations had legitimately, through renewal chapters, changed directives on this question. The SCRIS promulgated and circulated a lengthy statement giving its opinion on the question of religious dress. The statement was sent to the then president of the NCCB, who in turn circulated it to every bishop of the United States. It was only after excerpts from this statement had been printed in the newspapers that Sister Betty Carroll requested and received a copy of the opinion from the president of the NCCB. In turn, Betty sent it to every member of the LCWR, and after about a month's time sent her personal reflections to the Conference on the opinion. The above experience, although eight years old, is still relevant. Several congregations in submitting constitutions were apprised that they will not be approved unless reference is given to religious dress and some statement indicating that it be worn at some time.

The question of religious dress has become a serious point of tension between women's communities and the institutional church. Pressures to regulate dress will continue to heighten such tensions.

2. In 1972–73 Sister Margaret Brennan was president of the Leadership Conference of Women Religious and was valiant in her efforts to keep dialogue open between the LCWR and the Consortium. She along with other officers travelled to Rome, as requested, in order that dialogue might ensue among the LCWR, the Consortium, and SCRIS. Margaret's special desire was to see the Holy Father, Pope Paul VI, for the sole purpose of receiving a blessing for the Leadership Conference. It was Margaret Brennan's sense of fidelity that prompted her to request such an audience. Margaret attempted for almost a year and a half to obtain such an audience, but none was ever granted.

3. With similar sentiments of concern for our church, I submitted two requests for some representatives of the LCWR to meet with Pope John Paul II. The first acknowledgment of this request came to me through the apostolic delegate, who had received a letter from the secretary of state. The second request has not yet been acknowledged.

I submit respectfully that the women's issue in the Roman Catholic Church is not, and cannot be, an isolated issue. The exclusion of women from the church as a system is a root evil and a social sin which must be eradicated if women are to be engaged in the institutional church. I am concerned for the growing number of women who have left the Roman Catholic Church and for those among us, both sisters and laywomen, who can no longer enter into the sacramental life of the church because of the sin of sexism. As women within the Roman Catholic system, we need to be in close union with laywomen so that together we can work and search for a church system which is more just. When we address the social sins of sexism and paternalism in the institutional church it is essential to distinguish persons from systems. The challenge to women is to address directly the evils within the systems and yet retain a compassionate stance toward the persons who may be involved either consciously or unconsciously in perpetuating the sinfulness.

## To Speak the Truth in Love to Our Society

The same social sin which lies at the base of the institutional church also forms the base for the institutional society. Although society, at least Western society, does not systemically exclude women, paternalism and sexism dominate society. At the recent UN Women's Conference in Copenhagen, the Secretariat for the conference extracted data to reveal a depressing reality. Of the 800 million illiterate persons in the world, two-thirds of them are women. Worldwide, women represent 51 percent of the population and 35 percent of the official labor force. Women perform for nearly 66 percent of all working hours, receive only 10 percent of the world's income, and own less than 1 percent of the world's property. These facts alone display the societal abuses committed against half of God's human family. Whenever and wherever persons are being exploited and the aspirations of humankind are subservient to profit, greed, and domination, Christians have a serious responsibility to speak truth. We, as women who stand among the battered, the abused, the victimized must speak truth in love to our society. No longer can we as women bring the good news of the Kingdom unless we are convinced that our sisters and brothers of this universe need to be approached as dignified, reverent adult women and men equal in the sight of God before any Gospel message can be taught.

For the limited time remaining I wish to highlight three areas that need personal and corporate reflection from us as women, as leaders of our respective congregations, and as the LCWR. I will speak only briefly to these topics; perhaps the coming days will give us an opportunity to elaborate on them.

## 1. The "return to prayer" syndrome

Throughout the past few years the statement that there has been a return to prayer, particularly among sisters, has been reiterated. It is as if the years following Vatican Council II had been a time to escape from prayer into hectic activity. This I do not believe was the situation. The changes in religious communities grew from reflections and experiences which were motivated and directed by personal and corporate prayer. We cannot allow the return to prayer syndrome to become a distraction nor an escape from the serious problems that confront us in the institutional church and in the institutional society. The call to action on behalf of justice and participation in the transformation of the world is a constitutive dimension of the preaching of the Gospel. It does not connote any return to a privatized spirituality. It obliges us to integrate spirituality and justice as two aspects of one reality. Spirituality without justice is a privatized religion. Justice without spirituality denies the inherent dignity and reverence due to every person created by God. Only continued attempts to integrate justice and spirituality will blend the personal and social dimensions of the Gospel.

## 2.   The need to rejuvenate the missionary spirit of our apostolic services.

Many women religious came to the United States to care for the immigrant church. They set about doing what was essential to forward the missionary activity. For many in the United States this meant establishing schools, hospitals, and social service facilities. The intention of our predecessors was not to erect buildings solely, but to do whatever was essential for the missionary service. Today, when two-thirds of the world's population live below subsistence level, women are again being challenged by the overwhelming needs of the poor and the oppressed to respond anew. Today we who are women religious need to de-institutionalize ourselves to become missionaries once again. The young women entering our religious congregations need ministerial experiences with the very poor people both in and outside of the United States. We need to be concerned if many women entering our congregations express a desire to be in middle-class institutional, educational, and health ministries. The concentration of women religious in the United States, and especially on the East Coast, is not a witness to a global consciousness; it is not a witness to the overwhelming needs of the poor and the oppressed in the Third and Fourth Worlds. There needs to be a redistribution of woman power if we are to be in solidarity with the poor and the marginated of our society. This call may even cause many to step outside of the established systems, to eventually withdraw from traditionally based ministries such as Catholic schools and health systems.

### 3. The need to denounce war as a form of institutionalized violence

For many years the social encyclicals of the church have addressed this serious societal evil. Yet we find that as Catholics, especially here in the United States, the issues of registration and draft, which came to our attention during this past year, found us discussing calmly and logically whether young men should be obliged to register or whether registration should also be extended to young women. War is one of the highest forms of institutionalized violence. The initiation and perpetuation of war is directly related to and affected by inflation and unemployment as well as rampant violence and crime in the streets and continued poverty and destitution for most of humanity. Vatican II and the social encyclicals challenged us not only to look at the effects of evil but to look also at the roots of evil. As women, as Christians, as members of the Leadership Conference, are we willing to denounce registration, draft, war and all its evil consequences? Are we willing to be known as women for peace and commit ourselves to promote a peaceful, nonviolent stance in every facet of life?

### Conclusion

I leave the fruits of my reflections to your ponderings, to the dialogue and interaction which will follow during the days ahead. As I conclude my remarks, I pray that some of my reflections may serve as catalysts to stimulate serious dialogue during this Assembly and throughout the coming year. Together as adults, together as women, together as Christian persons, let us fearlessly, joyously, and enthusiastically forge ahead into the 1980s, realizing that every facet of our ministerial lives has personal and social dimensions before God and humankind. We have been created to live on this earth for a brief span of time with other persons, striving to live in integrity and reverence with all who comprise the human family. It is through the continued quest for a life of interior freedom and personal integrity that God our creator, redeemer, and sanctifier will be fully present, continually revealing herself-himself to and through us. We who are redeemed yet sinful, strong yet weak, and infinite through our finiteness, render fidelity to God by struggling to be instruments of justice and peace through a life characterized by truth and charity.

"Let us profess the truth in love and grow to the full maturity of Christ."

# 3

*1985 National Assembly*
*"Women at the Well"*
*(Women as Moral Decision Makers)*

# THE WOMAN'S WORD
# OF TESTIMONY

## *Margaret Cafferty, PBVM*

— New Orleans, September 5, 1985 —

By the mid-1980s, Margaret Cafferty was able to draw upon the events
of the day, particularly the violent conflicts in Central America, to paint a
clear and uncompromising picture of the role and responsibilities of women
religious leaders in a world where the power of the United States continued
to cast a long shadow over world affairs.

Assassins succeeded in murdering Egypt's president, India's prime
minister, and four church women in El Salvador, but failed in attempts
on the U.S. president and the pope. Britain and Argentina went to war
over the Falklands while Argentine human rights groups unearthed atroci-
ties of the Dirty War. South Africa's president lifted the ban on interracial
marriages and considered expanding the voice of blacks; a South African
bishop accepted the Nobel Peace Prize; and elsewhere on that continent
drought, famine, and death stalked the poor. Martial law banned Solidarity in Poland, and the Irish Republican Army pursued its guerrilla warfare
against Britain. Iran invaded Iraq during the same year that the Iran-
Contra scandal erupted in the United States. Early cases of a new malady
called AIDS swiftly escalated into a deadly pandemic.

The Quinn Commission established listening sessions in response to
two documents: the April 1983 papal letter to the U.S. bishops requesting

28

*"special pastoral service" to religious communities and their declining num-*
*bers, and the May 1983* Essential Elements in the Church's Teaching
on Religious Life *from SCRIS. The Vatican demanded retraction from*
*certain individuals who signed a* New York Times *ad calling for dialogue*
*in the church on abortion. Physicist Sally Ride became the first Ameri-*
*can woman in space, and a U.S. plan for a missile shield was quickly*
*dubbed "Star Wars." The United States and others sent "peacekeeping"*
*troops into Lebanon, U.S. forces invaded the island of Granada, and the*
*Vietnam Memorial dedication honored the dead from the more than two*
*decades of that conflict.*

*Naming the questions facing the human community as religious ques-*
*tions, this address is the testimony of women speaking words of peace,*
*justice, and equality to a cherished nation and a beloved church—both of*
*which seemed to lack ears to hear.*

When storyteller John Shea begins his narrative of what transpired
between Jesus and the Samaritan woman at Jacob's well, he warns:
"Let those who have ears to hear, hear this story. Let those who have
eyes to see, see this scene. Anything can happen at a well."

In the Gospel of John's story of the Samaritan woman at the
well, lives touched, compassion flowed, water was exchanged, and
woman, evangelized, became evangelizer.

During this past week we have been gathered as women at a
well, drawing on wellsprings of common experience, sharing stories,
learning from one another, tightening the threads that weave us to
sisterhood. Our lives have touched, our vision has been stretched
and challenged, and compassion has flowed.

Perhaps more than any recent Assembly, this 1985 gathering
has called the membership of the Leadership Conference of Women
Religious to look at some of the complex, difficult questions and
issues we as religious, women, and leaders face in our times—questions related to both church and nation, questions we probably could
not have framed or expressed a few decades ago, questions that then
might not even have appeared religious.

Perhaps the most sobering and gratifying aspect of the Assembly is not that we have formulated answers for either society or church, but that we as religious are asking the profound questions facing the human community, that it is clear to us that those are religious questions, and that those questions are intimately related to our mission today:

- When, because of technology, our society and even we can do almost anything, what are we morally impelled to do?

- What must we do first, and for whom?

- Of what we can do, what must we never do, or stand silently by and allow others to do?

- When is silence an unspeakable sin?

- When all the choices are bad, what shall we do?

This well gathering, like all the experiences of our lives, has called us to ask hard questions of ourselves, to look at how we form our consciences and make decisions. It has called us to the continuing process of conversion, and we leave evangelized and evangelizer. Our word of testimony is that the message of the Gospel is relevant to our times. Our mission is shaped by the needs of the human community, by God suffering in our world.

We may share this mission with all apostolic religious, but for us as North Americans, the mission is unique. In the past few years, like many of you, I have had the privilege of attending meetings of members of my own religious congregation from around the world. Each time, I have come home awed by how different religious life in the United States is—certainly different from India, Africa, Pakistan, but even very different from Australia, Ireland, and Canada. And I realize that becoming religious in a nation that is a world power, a nuclear power, a super power, makes us different.

Our nation is one of those responsible for the escalation of nuclear weapons. We have pursued that course while increasing unemployment, allowing our poor to become a permanent underclass, dismantling our social programs. We also bear major responsibility for the current turmoil in Central America, for snuffing out the hope of liberation and reinforcing the oppression of dictatorship. We rationalize "constructive engagement" with a nation bound to show that a mark of white supremacy is brutality more characteristic of barbarism than of advanced civilization.

Religious have reflected on these phenomena in the presence of a God who made creation holy; in the company of prophets who burned with zeal for the poor; before Jesus who counted sparrows and was gentle with the bruised reed; with foundresses who read their own times with a prophetic eye and courageous heart.

As a result of our experience and our reflection, we U.S. religious describe ourselves differently. Our need to be prophetic, our responsibility to be prophetic is different from that of religious in other parts of the world. We have a sense that our witness, our vows, our ministry must say something of the Gospel to our nation, to a nation that has the capacity and seemingly the will to destroy creation as we know it today.

Our relationship with the church is also different from that of other religious. We have been told on several occasions over the past two years that what U.S. religious are and do has a ripple effect on religious life all over the world because of our numbers, because so much in religious formation and renewal has begun here, because of the contribution religious have made to the development of faith in our own nation and, through our missionaries, to the faith throughout the world. And yet, in spite of all the significance placed on our lives, we are still unable to communicate to the wider church an appreciation of what we view as unique or valuable in our experience.

Because the issues of our time are so complex, because the implications of horrors like nuclear holocaust are so awesome, because the institutions we deal with appear unchangeable, it is easy to understand why people are overwhelmed, why they choose to drop out, why a generation of youth is convinced that creation is ugly, nuclear war inevitable, and the only moment worth celebrating is now.

Most of us entered religious life because we wanted our lives to count for something. We wanted to live them for something significant. These are times when those who live with purpose can and must make a difference. If there is anything our coming together these days should have convinced us of, it is that there are times when the only moral choice is to speak, to act. We live in such times.

If the mission of Jesus was in part to create here and now a human dwelling place worthy of the sacredness of creation and the human family, our lives, our ministry extend that mission through time. Part of that mission today, part of the mission of the Gospel is to speak the word of peace to our nation.

The making of peace is probably the greatest challenge facing humanity today. In a recent TV special, a commentator defined peace as the interval between wars; peace, the pause; war, the normal human activity. In this nation, we have a new vocabulary, a kind of doublespeak that George Orwell predicted would be the vernacular by 1984:

- A missile that deals death and destruction is called peacekeeper.

- National budget priorities that have put more people at risk, especially more women and children, than at any other time since the Great Depression are set for reasons of national security.

- Arms sales that impoverish the Third World are called development.

- A marauding army that tortures and murders innocent civilians is dubbed freedom fighters.

- A Steven Speilberg orgy of violence is singled out as a model for how a civilized nation might conduct itself in times of international crisis, and *Rambo, First Blood* becomes the All-American hero.

During this past August, it was sobering for our nation to recall that there have been not one, but two holocausts in modern history. One took place over a period of years in the ovens and death camps of Germany, the other in a split second under the mushroom clouds of Hiroshima and Nagasaki.

As women who spend much of our lives nurturing the young and caring for the aged, who know both the pain and the beauty of birth and of death, we must not let our nation forget to weep at the horror of holocaust, nor to ask, "Are we robbing the children of the future?"

The LCWR made a commitment to peacemaking in 1981. One of the heartening experiences of assembling the annual Conference report is reviewing the reports of individual regions and realizing how that commitment to peace has permeated the activity of every region, and, I dare say, of nearly every religious congregation from formation house to infirmary.

During the past year, religious have lobbied hard and consistently against spending for nuclear weapons. They have taught about, reflected on, and organized around the causes of war and the demands of peace; they helped wrap the Pentagon in miles of things they could not bear to see destroyed in a nuclear holocaust; they have declared their mother houses nuclear-free zones; they have prayed and fasted and gone to prison for peace.

Religious women in the United States met a unique need in earlier times. They helped to educate an immigrant nation and to build the church in the United States. Perhaps the greatest contribution we can make to this, our time, is to help shape the conscience of this nation, to build a people who will not tolerate the blasphemy of destroying creation.

*We must speak the word of justice to our nation, paticularly the word of justice for the nations of Central America.*

Why should Central America, above all corners of the world, be a concern to us? Because it is here in our own hemisphere, in our own backyard, almost within driving distance. Because the focus of persecution in most of the countries of Central America is the church, a church that has made itself the enemy because of its option for the poor, because of taking renewal seriously, because of responding to the Gospel. Because we have missioned our own sisters to Central America. Because through our missionaries we probably have more firsthand information about Central America than any other organization in North America.

Each year, I visit the missions of my own community in Nicaragua, Guatemala, and Mexico. In every country, people forgive me for being North American before they can talk to me as a person, and in every country ordinary people, mothers, young soldiers, catechists, teenagers come up to me and ask, "Why is your country doing this to us?"

In Nicaragua, a teenager who should have been in school studying engineering but who was fighting his second war asked, "Can't you tell the people in the United States what your government is really doing?" A mother who had lost her husband and sons in the current Nicaraguan war said, "Your government can kill all the young men and all the old men. Then the women will fight." At a meeting of catechists in the jungle of southern Mexico on the margins of the world, an Indian leader stood and asked, "Why is your government aiding an army that is killing our Guatemalan brothers and sisters?" There is nowhere in Latin America a North American can go and escape the judgment of the poor.

When LCWR representatives returned from the meeting of the Confederation of Latin American Religious in Guatemala in April, they brought home with them a letter from the religious of El Salvador saying that the deaths of four U.S. missionary women in 1980 had been a seed for the development of faith in El Salvador, especially among young people. The letter was an expression of profound gratitude for the gift of life from Maura, Ita, Jean, and Dorothy, from whom new life flows in a suffering, indigenous church.[1] The CLAR membership at this same meeting agreed that the situation in Guatemala is now the most repressive and dangerous in all of Latin America; religious from Guatemala testified that U.S. missionaries are among the most dedicated, willing to risk their lives to accompany the people in their struggle for liberation.

The struggle for justice in Central America has spilled across our borders into the United States, with a stream of refugees seeking sanctuary. In growing numbers, religious congregations are opening their homes to refugees, opening their consciences to their stories.

Few other groups in the United States have access to the privileged information we have, to the experience of our own sisters in Central America, and the experience of our sisters with refugees here in the United States. That experience is the occasion of conversion for us. We have given martyrs. Now we must give teachers and organizers, prophets and witnesses who will wage an unrelenting campaign for the right of the poor of Central America to shape their own destiny.

## *We speak the word of justice for women; we speak that word to nation and to church.*

It should surprise no one that the plight of women is a special concern for U.S. religious. How can we take seriously the Gospel call for justice and exempt from that call half of humanity? How can we take seriously the Gospel assertion of the dignity of every human person and refuse to acknowledge that dignity in half the world's persons? Many of our religious congregations were first formed to meet the needs of specific groups of women: girls society refused to educate; orphaned girls who would otherwise have been forced into prostitution; widowed, aged, and ill women. As congregations continue to serve the unique needs of women, our consciences have been honed by the stories of poor women, battered and abused women, women who feel like undocumented persons in the male nation of the church.

The plight of women in the church reminds me of a set of definitions I read some years ago; the definitions were probably the work of an associate pastor. They are these:

*Bishop:* Leaps buildings in a single bound. Is more powerful than a locomotive. Is faster than a speeding bullet. Walks on water. Gives policy to God.

*Chancellor:* Leaps buildings with a running start and a favorable wind. Is almost as powerful as a switch engine. Is faster than a speeding BB. Walks on water in an indoor swimming pool. Talks with God if special request is approved.

*Pastor:* Makes high marks on the wall when trying to leap buildings. Is run over by a locomotive. Can sometimes handle a gun without inflicting self-injury. Dog paddles. Talks to anyone who will listen.

*Parish Secretary:* Lifts buildings and walks under them. Kicks locomotives off the tracks. Catches speeding bullets with her teeth and eats them. Freezes water with a single glance. She is God.

Women who struggle for recognition in the church claim neither divinity nor superiority. What they do demand is the freedom to exercise the gifts God has given them, gifts given for the good of the whole Christian community.

The current economic situation in this nation has put a new edge of urgency on the issue of women's rights. With increasing, alarming frequency, to be woman, child, or old in the United States means to be poor. To be black and woman means to be poorer.

We are appalled that in many cultures woman is still viewed simply as the bearer of water and provider of food, as the bearer of children, preferably male children. We should be equally appalled that in this nation, femininity condemns an increasing number of women to a life of poverty, with little hope of escape.

One concrete step LCWR members could take to address the growing injustice against women is to make legislation affecting women, especially legislation relating to poverty and economic opportunity, not only a priority for our time and effort, but a matter of conscience. For many of us, our concern for women today could more appropriately be called fidelity to our founding charism, rather than dismissed, as it often is, as a peculiarly religious brand of radical feminism. For all of us, it is a demand of our commitment to the Gospel.

## We must speak the word of justice to our church.

This is perhaps the most difficult of all the words we are called to give in testimony. The evolution of apostolic religious life in the United States is a unique phenomenon, shaped by the renewal of the entire church and by the history and culture of this nation. We have incorporated into our lives values that are uniquely North American. We have probably also incorporated some uniquely North American vices.

I personally welcome the challenge of belonging to a universal church. I want something larger than my subjective view of the truth by which I can measure and evaluate my experience. When my Latin or Asian sisters wince at my excessive individualism, I realize once again that my culture is flawed at its very best.

However, the North American experience has created good things, practices and institutions that have liberated the human spirit and fueled dreams over the world. These positive values may be more alive in our American myth than they are in our national institutions, but we have incorporated them into renewed religious life. Among them are respect for individual conscience, a respect for the value and the worth of the human person, a strong belief that justice cannot be done with an unjust process, an awakening sense of respect for the gifts and the dignity of women.

A truly universal church can only be enriched by recognizing that cultural diversity is real and that something of God is revealed in each unique culture. We U.S. religious have no monopoly on the truth, but we do lay claim to some of it. We simply ask for the privilege of sharing with the rest of the church what we know to be good, to be consistent with the Gospel. Above all, we ask for the privilege of ordering our own lives by those values. We are part of a current of church women extending from Teresa of Avila to Teresa of Mercy, who insist on the right to name and claim our own experience.

*And so we speak our words of testimony:*
*words of peace, of justice, of equality, of experience.*

The testimony we offer is not a quiet, private word, whispered in the corners of individual hearts. It is a public word, shouted in the strength of our witness and in the vitality of our ministry, for the time in which we live demands more than personal piety.

These times, our times, could probably best be described as transitional. We are evolving to a new expression of apostolic religious life; we are testing new ways of relating to our society and to the church. We are still much closer to a certain, recent past than we are to an elusive future. It is time for hope, for trust in things unseen, for planting seedlings that will grow to shade the justice and peace of future generations.

When Marie Augusta Neal did her study of apostolic religious life in 1966, one of the questions she asked was "What do you think is most needed in religious life today?" Close to half the respondents replied, "Circumspection and patience."

When Neal did her follow-up study in 1982, circumspection and patience had plummeted to 7 percent. The times we live in may indeed have greater need of imagination, risk, and daring than of patience.

We face them in the company of foundresses who risked the French guillotine and Irish Penal Laws, the rigors of the wild North American West and the misunderstanding of the church to follow the summons of a beckoning Spirit. We face them with a Lord who begged water from an outcast Samaritan woman, and who took time to listen to her experience. That same Lord urges us on, reminding us that the fields are gleaming white, all ready for the harvest.

### Notes

1. In December 1980 four North American church women were murdered by soldiers in El Salvador. They were Maryknoll Sisters Maura Clarke and Ita Ford, Ursuline Sister Dorothy Kazel, and Jean Donovan, a lay missioner from Cleveland.

# 4

*1989 Joint National Assembly*
*with Conference of Major Superiors of Men*
*"Wondrous Road by Starry Flame"*

# CONSECRATED FOR MISSION

## *Nadine Foley, OP*

— Louisville, August 1989 —

*"The present,"* Nadine Foley, OP, *noted in addressing the LCWR membership in August 1989, "is rooted in the past, and the future is somehow contained in the present." Events leading up to that moment witnessed unmistakably to the truth of these words.*

*Decades of Communist rule in Eastern Europe were coming to an end as the Baltic states took the first faltering steps toward freeing themselves from Soviet occupation. In Poland, Solidarity was entering candidates in national elections, and the leader of Romania and his wife were executed for the crime of genocide. Palestine declared itself independent within a year of the first intifada against the State of Israel. Soviet troops exited from Afghanistan, and in mainland China a lone protester faced down a tank in Tiananmen Square. In Nicaragua the Sandinista government and the contras called a truce, while in Myanmar the government placed dissident Aung San Suu Kyi under house arrest. A bomb on Pan Am Flight 103 detonated in midair, and the U.S. Challenger spacecraft exploded during liftoff. Tens of thousands perished in a massive earthquake in Mexico. The Chernobyl nuclear reactor disaster transformed a large swath of Russian countryside into a nuclear wasteland.*

*In the United States the Catholic bishops published their pastoral letter* Economic Justice for All, *while theologian Charles Curran was removed from his teaching position at Catholic University for voicing dissent on the church's teaching about birth control. The LCWR continued its dialogue with the leaders of* Consortium Perfectae Caritatis. *LCWR collaboration with bishops and men religious deepened through the newly formed Tri-Conference Commission. The LCWR and the Conference of Major Superiors of Men (CMSM) worked together to identify ten "transformative elements" that describe how leaders see religious life.*

*In language that seeks to embrace and influence rather than divide and control, this address highlights the witness of women religious through consecration, mission, feminism, and justice.*

There are two questions, it seems to me, around which we gather much interest, energy, and concern these days. One is "What is the future of religious life?"—with the attendant question for some, "What will be its new forms?" The other, to which we often come as we explore the first, is, "What is religious life?" Both questions are raised too by others than ourselves, particularly by church leaders faced with an uncertain future as to how the work of the church will be furthered in the confusing and distressing social, religious, and moral climate of our times. For the latter there is often the conviction that religious life has lost its moorings, so to speak, that it has lost faith with its true nature as a charism given by God to the church.

These questions have historical dimensions, obviously. The present is rooted in the past, and the future is somehow contained in the present. As we have experienced the development of religious life in our unique U.S. history, we know that there is a continuum of values that has perdured in continuity with the most ancient forms of religious life and the aspirations of those who have lived them out. In our own milieu, through the more than two hundred years since women religious came to these shores, religious life has had its own history of adaptation and accommodation. Truly great women, with vision, courage, and determination, with uncompromising love for people and the church, made the Gospel a living presence in an alien environment—alien in the hardships of frontier life and alien in an atmosphere of antipathy and distrust of Catholicity.

Current historians are gradually bringing to light the contributions to the growth of the U.S. church by women like Mother Joseph Periseau, SP; Mother Austin Carroll, RSM; Mother Philippine Duchesne, RSCJ; Mother Bernadine Cabaret, SCSA; Sister Joanna Brunner, SCL; Mother St. John Fournier, SSJ; Mother Angela Gillespie, CSC, and countless others.[1] They and their like in all our congregations served the poor through education and health care, not only the affluent but Native Americans and blacks. They started schools and hospitals, but also soup kitchens, day-care centers, and dispensaries, initiated prison ministries and extended themselves to prostitutes and other destitute women, responded to victims of earthquakes, floods, and epidemics and nursed on the battlefields of our wars.

These women were generally not theorists about what religious life is, nor did they have conferences on the future of religious life, as far as I know. They were practitioners of the Gospel. But to be what they needed to be they were at the same time architects of religious life in a new form, an active ministerial form that in some cases grew out of the monastic and mendicant traditions of their European motherhouses. In other instances they were products of new congregations, brought into being specifically for active ministerial service, sometimes for specific kinds of apostolates.

Yet often there were struggles in which the lines were quite clearly drawn. The Carmelites who came to Port Tobacco, Charles County, Maryland, in 1790, were successful in holding on to their contemplative life despite pressures placed upon them to engage in an active ministry of education. The Dominican Sisters agonized over the option to forsake their second-order status for a more flexible third-order modality, but finally chose the latter as more adaptable to their active ministries.

There were numerous local conflicts like that of Mother Rose Kempter, sent from the East to take charge of a small hospital in the Midwest. There she admitted an unwed mother and delivered her infant. She also accepted the day-old child of another unwed mother. The local pastor requested her removal, and charity was out-weighed by caution in this instance, but happily not in many others.[2] The heroic work of Mother Austin Carroll in the South was called into question by local clergy and the bishop, and charges were made in Rome. The controversy waged for years before it was resolved. At the root of the issues was what was appropriate or seemly conduct of sisters in the ministry and vis-à-vis the clergy.

The spirit of the sisters was one of adaptation in response to the experienced needs of the times and circumstances. It is evident in the words of a religious superior who wrote to one of her sisters who headed a hospital unit during the Civil War:

> I suppose that you will be dispensed of a part of your prayers, and even Mass and Holy Communion through the week. Make a good meditation in the morning. Offer up all the actions of the day, attend to those poor people, and I think Our Lord will be satisfied.[3]

Questions about the nature of religious life were around in those earlier times, and some now familiar ploys were used to con-tain the spirit-filled zeal of our pioneer foremothers, even, I regret to say, reducing their salaries. It was a time when there was only one approved form of religious life for women, and the tension was often that between what "ought to be," as some perceived it, and what the missionary needs were for a new and developing way of life in a new world. The sisters themselves experienced the strain as they continued to follow the daily regimen of monastic observance while carrying on their active work. The toll in broken health and early death was drastic for many of these women.

While the active ministerial form of religious life for women received formal ecclesial recognition at the turn of the twentieth century and was incorporated in the 1917 Code of Canon Law, it did little to address the fundamental nature of what was developing. It is my contention that only in the post–Vatican II period, as we have tried to articulate our self-understanding emerging from our experience, have we begun to formulate in words who we have become as active ministerial women religious in our multifaceted U.S. society and cultures and in the extension of our ministries globally. We have done so in chapter enactments over the past twenty-five years and in new constitutions and statutes. And it is interesting that in the process we have revived old controversies and contentions. Now it seems that we may be coming to a kind of impasse despite some signs of evident progress.

Earlier this summer I read Margaret O'Brien Steinfels's article in *America*, "The Church and Its Public Life."[4] Her thesis—that in the public life of the church there is a crisis of language evident in the gap between words and reality—has served for me as a focal point for synthesizing some recent experiences and impressions. To the extent that we women religious belong to the public life of the church, and we do, there is, I believe, a crisis of language in our effort to carry on dialogue. While words should be a medium of communication and understanding, I believe that there are instances at hand in which they are used in a manner that furthers separation and alienation in the current questioning about the nature of religious life. I would like to single out four: mission and consecration, radical feminism, and compensation.

## Mission and Consecration

How frequently now we hear the words "mission" and "consecration" applied to the life of women religious as distinctive categories that separate one group from another. It is a curiosity that these words are emerging as class names for different types of women's religious life. In his presentation at the summation meeting of the U.S. bishops in Rome last March, Cardinal Hickey described two types of religious life. He said, "The focus on mission seems characteristic of the majority of religious institutes of men and women in the United States." And further, "A second approach focuses on consecration through the vows as a value in itself and as a basis for community apostolate."[5]

The distinction is also pointed out in the letter of Pope John Paul II to the U.S. bishops. He says, "The study of the Pontifical Commission and your own letters point out an apparent tension between consecration and mission. The centrality of the evangelical counsels must continue to be emphasized. Consecrated life of its very nature is linked to the profession and living of consecrated chastity, poverty, and obedience. Religious are not merely clerical or lay persons dedicated to good works."[6]

A quotation from *Perfectae Caritatis* follows to the effect that "the whole religious life of the members should be inspired by an apostolic spirit and all their apostolic activity formed by the spirit of religion."

The implication of what we read here is that to emphasize mission in expressing our identity as active ministerial religious congregations is somehow to negate the notion of consecration, identified with the vows. And yet I do not find these concepts in opposition to one another. In fact I would hold that there is good biblical foundation for believing that the whole people of God, the church, is consecrated for mission through baptism. And if the profession of vows is an intensification of baptism, then it follows that the same profession of vows is an intensification of the consecration for mission incumbent on all the baptized.

My reference is the Gospel of John, chapter 17, verses 17–19. It is the last discourse of Jesus to his disciples, and he prays: "Consecrate them by means of truth—'Your word is truth.' As you have sent me into the world, so I have sent them into the world: I consecrate myself for their sakes now, that they may be consecrated in truth."

As Raymond Brown says in his commentary on this text, "The consecration in truth is not simply a purification from sin but is a consecration to a mission: they are being consecrated inasmuch as they are being sent."[7] Another commentator on the same text says that "the locus for God's words and works in the era of Jesus is the brothers and the sisters" who "can carry on the Father's plan to challenge and hopefully save the world by announcing the plan and living it before the world."[8] And still another says, "When Christ prays for his disciples that they may be sanctified and consecrated in the truth John is probably not thinking of a select few who will be ministerial priests and sacrificial victims, but of a consecration to his own mission by all disciples."[9]

The relationship between consecration and mission in this important text is undeniable. This means a critical realization for some of us who may be uncomfortable with the word "consecration."

The issue is one of theology. The common meaning of being consecrated is "separated from common life or use and dedicated in some way to the service or worship of God."[10] In a dualistically informed theology, consecration can emphasize the sense of separation, and we all know how that meaning was incorporated into the theology of religious life. We became signs and symbols by our way of life, which often incorporated archaic and meaningless practices, our manner of dress and behavior, and our enclosures. We were to bear eschatological witness to these ways, and our ministerial endeavors were perceived to be secondary, even perhaps forms of personal asceticism. Such ideas were frequently in tension with our sense of mission carried out in active ministerial service.

In our zeal for renewal, for affirming the validity of our mission-oriented, active ministerial involvement with our contemporary world, we may have too easily de-emphasized the word "consecration." While it may mean one thing in one theological context, it can take on new nuances of interpretation in another. In the discourse of Jesus, as recorded in John's Gospel, the active consecration by Jesus is essential to the character of his missioned disciples.

We need not be uncomfortable with the notion of consecration, then, if we understand it in the context of the biblical, incarnational theology of John. We are indeed consecrated, sanctified, as among those who are joined into Jesus and his mission. We are part of the mystery of his ongoing presence and redemptive activity, a reality that draws us to constant reflective prayer. Along with all the baptized we are a missioned people. If we are separated, it is because we are to be separated from the spirit of the world to live in the spirit of Jesus under the impulse of the Holy Spirit.

In a similar manner we can understand the meaning of witness. In these years of renewal we have reflected much upon some time-honored interpretations of religious life. The idea that by our dress and lifestyle we were to be "eschatological signs," even if we never did anything that seemed significant, was not a particularly attractive idea as we thought about it. But eschatological sign in the sense of incarnating the real possibility of the Reign of God, through our activity on behalf of justice and peace, is equivalent to being living, active, effective signs of what it was that Jesus came to accomplish. We deny that possibility at the risk of denying our identity as Christian disciples. But if we affirm it, we must realize the enormousness of the challenge and the responsibility of being in truth what we say we are.

Those of us who are vowed members of religious institutes are called to be witnesses. We intensify our baptismal consecration in order to be sign and facilitator, to the degree that we can, of the missionary potential of all the baptized. We are called to be among the people of God, in service for them and with them, marked by our passion for bringing about the Reign of God.

Therein lies our witness: to be visible by the intensity of our unique commitment to the mission of Jesus in vowed communities of ministerial service. We are consecrated for mission in active ministerial communities, and mission is our witness. We are ultimately to be sources of unity and reconciliation in all that we do and so to further the coming of the Reign of God. In that sense, along with all the faithful, we can and must be eschatological witnesses.

I find these ideas contained in the document entitled *Religious and Human Promotion*, issued by the SCRIS in 1980. While such ideas are pervasive in this text, the following captures the spirit of what is said:

> Religious know that they are caught up daily in a path of conversion to the kingdom of God, which makes them in the Church and before the world a sign capable of attracting, thus inspiring a profound revision of life and values.

This is, without doubt, the most needed and fruitful commitment to which they are called, even in those areas where the Christian community works for human promotion and for the development of social relations inspired by principles of solidarity and [fraternal] communion.

In this way, they cooperate in "safeguarding the originality of Christian liberation and the energies that it is capable of developing—liberation in its full, profound sense, as Jesus proclaimed and accomplished it."

By spreading in this way the Christian and profoundly human meaning of the realities of history, which finds its origin in the beatitudes which have now become the criterion for life, religious show how close is the bond between the Gospel and human promotion in social coexistence. For this reason, the church can point to the evangelical witness of religious as a splendid and singular proof that the way of the beatitudes is the only one capable of "transforming this world and offering it to God."[11]

This document deserves to be reread by those who find it difficult to reconcile the notions of consecration and mission, or who use them to segregate and divide. We are consecrated for mission, and we need to claim that identity for those who pioneered that reality in the arduous circumstances of the past and for the sake of our continuing relevance as women religious in our equally difficult contemporary world. We, and others with us, need to reject the false dichotomy between consecration and mission and to understand how fully the vows and the mission are in accord.

## Radical Feminism

We women religious are not the only ones who have been cited as proponents of "radical feminism." But, while the term has not been defined in the ecclesiastical circles in which it is current, we have been singled out for our concerns with feminist issues precisely because it is perceived as incongruous that women religious should have an interest in the feminist agendas. Here again language is invoked to divide, separate, and control. And the issue of what is religious life is invoked again.

Margaret Steinfels is right when she says that "the current use of 'radical feminism' closes rather than opens discussion, uses a label to convict without either indentifying the accused or arguing the case. . . . Incantation of the phrase "radical feminism" may persuade some church officials that they have found the magic formula for staving off unwelcome claims. But rather than persuading plain feminists to give up their claims, it is more likely to persuade them that they are radical feminists."[12]

I suspect that among women religious there is a wide spectrum of attitudes within the scope of what we call "feminism." The term admits of a basic generic meaning, that is, "a theory or doctrine about women." In that sense, anyone who has a set of ideas about women is some kind of a feminist. The issue then becomes not whether or not one is a feminist, because probably every thinking person is some kind of feminist, but rather what kind of feminist one is. Sister Sandra Schneiders, IHM, has proposed that there are romantic, radical, liberal, and liberationist feminists. And there may be other sets of categories.

The issue for us as a Conference is whether or not it is consistent with our mandate to promote religious life to make "women's issues" one of our priorities in our ongoing agenda. Does feminism, as the label is being used, have any consonance with religious life, or is it totally extraneous? Is there something about the active ministerial religious life of women that renders it removed from what we call women's issues and the kind of feminist concern we have brought to bear upon them?

I would hesitate to call the activities of our Conference in women's issues over the last fifteen years expressive of a radical position on feminism, according to my understanding. I would place them, rather, within the ambit of activities bearing upon the promotion of active ministerial religious life. While we have not been concerned merely with ourselves, it is nonetheless important that we are attentive to how our potential for Gospel ministry can be maximized and to how forces within our society and church oppress and dehumanize. Thus our goal on women has both an internal and an external focus.

We women religious are women, a group within the larger set of women in the church. We have not eschewed our womanhood by entering into a vowed religious life. What we have done is to bring the "feminine," or "partnership" view of human relations,[13] and its unique consciousness, to the arena of church ministry. And what we most desire is to find the ways to render it truly effective both within the church and in the society wherein we carry on our active ministerial work even at the risk of being labeled tenderhearted. We want this because we care about the church, we care about its public image, we care about its extension in ministry to all human beings, and we care that within its own makeup it reflects the universal effect of salvation that Jesus accomplished.

The church is a patriarchy. To say that is not to espouse a position of "radical feminism." It is to state a self-evident fact. And to say that therefore the church is flawed is to interface that fact with the message of Jesus. In our contemporary era of biblical insight and understanding, there is enough scholarly evidence to question some of the long-standing assumptions about the exclusivity of Jesus' call to only male disciples. The challenge now to us and to our church is to have the courage to internalize the full message of the Gospel and to transform the church so that it is a credible witness to that Gospel. None of us is so naïve as to think that the church as a functioning "discipleship of equals"[14] can be accomplished overnight. But, with bold assertive initiatives taken in the present, that reality can be assured for the future. I have no doubt that we women religious will continue to take them, as our foremothers did, but we live in the hope that we can do so with our codisciples in the church.

The document *Religious and Human Promotion* says that "to establish the kingdom of God within the very structures of the world, insofar as this constitutes evangelical promotion in human history, is certainly a theme of great interest for the whole Christian community, and therefore for religious also." And in this context it continues:

> It is from this point of view that the efforts of women religious to cooperate in the advancement of women are to be encouraged, so that women may succeed in being involved in those areas of public and ecclesial life which best correspond with their particular nature and the qualities that are proper to them.[15]

While we have an ongoing critique of the theory of women's "particular nature" and "proper" qualities, this statement nonetheless affirms our conviction about why we need to be involved in women's issues as active ministerial women religious. It is the fundamental insight of our so-called feminism. But it is important to say that we do not pursue women's issues as an isolated agenda. We pursue them within the spectrum of social and political concerns on a global scale and we urge our codisciples in the church to do the same.

## Compensation

A third word emerging in the current discourse about what is religious life is "compensation." We have looked to the past, to how we might meet past liability for current retirement, and we have had the extraordinary response of the people of God to the appeal generated through Tri-Conference Commission collaboration. The next phase is to look to the present in light of the future and to offset the continuance of the problem through adequate compensation. Adequate compensation, as we would define it, is compensation sufficient to meet our current living requirements, our future retirement needs, our expenses for formation and education in our congregations, for administration, and for the support of our ministries to the disadvantaged at home and abroad.

Curiously, once again, as we have attempted to address the issues, a point of view had developed that to compensate religious, as we define our needs, is somehow contrary to the vow of poverty and therefore incompatible with an authentic religious life. Last year

Sister Andre Fries, CPPS, addressed this question with us and suggested that compensation has taken on a symbolic significance for religious life, that to pursue adequate compensation as we perceive it is to obliterate the distinctive difference between religious and members of the laity.

The expression "self-serving" has been used. Appeals to a romanticized and nostalgic past, when religious did not make such demands, have been heard. It was precisely such a past, when we were young and growing and unconcerned about how to provide for ourselves in a seemingly distant future, that has compounded the present for us. That past, after all, had some inglorious features as we, and the church, literally scrounged to keep our active works alive. I can't resist quoting from a letter of a major superior who had occasion to write to the monsignor who was superintendent of schools in a large archdiocese as follows:

> This racketeering for money in the schools is the weightiest problem I have, and what I write now concerning it I am intrusting [sic] to you in strictest confidence. You know as well as I do that the Sisters are at the present time just sublimated "hucksters" clothed in the Religious Habit. I not only abhor the abuse, but I fear the grave consequences that commercialism will bring to Christianity . . . I know that none of this is new to you or due to you, but I know you can be a power in removing some causes and I want you to be sure that I am willing to sacrifice anything. I am thinking not only of our Community, but the church. I know many things that we shall have to correct as far as our Sisters are concerned, but I know that it will need a stronger force than I can provide to correct the abuse and remove the causes from other sources. I know that we who embrace the vows must and can certainly live healthy lives with the salary that should be provided for us by the parishes, as well as I know that these sales, parties, and other activities that make the Sisters tyrants in the classroom, wrenching money and

embarrassing the children that they came to "instruct unto justice," can be discharged by adult organizations. It seems to me that you will take a step in the right direction to correct this so that the Sisters, free from the bonds of money-making, can be restored to the dignity of Christian teachers seeking "first the kingdom of heaven."[16]

It is not my purpose to generalize from this letter. But its implicit appeal for dignity and for personal and communal independence in carrying out the ministry is the fundamental issue in today's pursuit of adequate compensation. It is inconceivable that it be compounded with questions of how many candidates some congregations have, or who has been most responsible in the use of their resources, or whether or not women religious can be trusted to use funds for the common good and for the mission. Nor need we draw the conclusion that women religious will refuse to serve those who cannot provide adequate compensation. The record both of the past and the present refutes any such claim.

Adequate compensation is a simple question of justice. It falls within the ambit of the principle laid down in the bishops' pastoral letter on the economy: "that those who serve the church—laity, clergy and religious—should receive a sufficient livelihood and the social benefits provided by responsible employers in our nation."[17]

## Conclusion

Underlying the many expressed concerns about consecration, mission, feminism, and compensation seem to be the questions about what is authentic religious life. I know, as you do, that that question is ours as well. And to our lives and our reflection upon them we have to bring an honest critique. We are the bearers of the charism of religious life and of its tradition lived out by our foremothers. We, and by "we" I mean all of our sisters, have the experience of active ministerial religious life in many arenas, and our contemporary reflection has brought us to a remarkable unanimity about its truth as an authentic form of religious life. We have reached a stage of maturity and comfort, I believe, when we can hear the honest questions of those who look at us with concern and when we can raise our own questions about whether and how we are preserving the inheritance we have received from the heroic women of our congregations in the past and in the present.

That questioning must be an ongoing part of our agendas. We do not know with certainty what the future will be. But we do know that its seeds are in the present and so we must be careful nurturers. For that we need the spirit of Wisdom to whom we can turn with confidence:

> For she is the refulgence of eternal light,
>   the spotless mirror of the power of God,
>   the image of his goodness.
> And she, who is one, can do all things,
>   and renews everything while herself perduring;
> And passing into holy souls from age to age,
>   she produces friends of God and prophets.

> (Wisdom 7:26–27)

Our foremothers were such friends of God and prophets. May we be worthy of their heritage entrusted to us.

## Notes

1. See Mary Ewens, "Women in the Convent," in *American Catholic Women*, ed. Karen Kennelly (New York: Macmillan, 1989), 17–47; and *Pioneer Healers*, ed. Ursula Stepsis and Dolores Liptak (New York: Crossroad, 1989).

2. Archives of the Adrian Dominican Sisters.

3. Stepsis and Liptak, eds., Quoted in *Pioneer Healers*, 44.

4. Margaret O'Brien Steinfels, "The Church and Its Public Life," *America* (June 10, 1989): 550–58.

5. *Origins* (March 23, 1989): 692

6. *Origins* (April 13, 1989): 747.

7. *The Gospel According to John*, Anchor Bible 29a (Garden City, NY: Doubleday, 1970), 762.

8. John M. J. Taylor, *The Different Gospel* (Staten Island, NY: Alba House, 1983), 211.

9. J. Wijngaards, *The Gospel of John and His Letters* (Wilmington, DE: Michael Glazier, 1986), 265.

10. *Eerdmans Bible Dictionary* (Grand Rapids: Eerdmans, 1987), 911.

11. Sacred Congregation for Religious and for Secular Institutes, *Religious and Human Promotion* (1981): 18, 19.

12. Steinfels, "The Church and Its Public Life," 554.

13. See Riane Eisler, *The Chalice and the Blade: Our History, Our Future* (San Francisco: Harper & Row, 1987), 151 These ideas are related to her proposal of *gylany* as a term connoting the linking of both halves of humanity (105ff).

14. The phrase is that of Elisabeth Schüssler Fiorenza and is developed in her book *In Memory of Her* (New York: Crossroad, 1984).

15. *Religious and Human Promotion*, 2, 3.

16. Mother Mary Gerald Barry, OP, January 8, 1937. Archives of the Adrian Dominican Sisters.

17. United States Catholic Bishops, *Economic Justice for All: Pastoral Letters on Catholic Social Teaching and the U.S. Economy* (1986), 351.

# 5

# BEFRIENDING THE WIND

## *Doris Gottemoeller, RSM*

— Chicago, August 29, 1994 —

*In exploring the metaphor of wind in this presidential address, Doris Gotte-moeller articulates the unseen forces of change that have influenced religious life from its beginnings and into the closing decade of the twentieth century. Events of the early 1990s served not only as backdrop for this reflection; they also confirmed the urgency of response.*

Old structures crumbled both literally and figuratively: the Berlin Wall came down, the Soviet Union dissolved, and South African apartheid collapsed. Simmering quarrels escalated into armed conflicts: Operation Desert Storm in Iraq, the U.S. invasion of Panama, a military coup in Haiti, Hutu against Tutsi in Rwanda, and "ethnic cleansing" in the Balkans. The first woman president of Ireland was elected, and another became the first prime minister of Pakistan. Bill Clinton succeeded George H. W. Bush as the U.S. president. Hurricane Andrew swept through the southeastern United States, and an earthquake shook San Francisco. Early in the decade the Internet came into its own.

Six Jesuit priests and their housekeeper and her daughter were murdered in San Salvador. The Vatican established diplomatic relations with the State of Israel, published a decree on ecumenism, and opened the first African synod of bishops in Rome. The Catechism of the Catholic Church was published, Galileo was rehabilitated, and a U.S. cardinal was falsely accused of sexual misconduct. The Church of England

*admitted women to the priesthood, and two years later a papal letter*
*affirmed that the Catholic Church "has no authority whatsoever to confer*
*priestly ordination on women." Doris Gottemoeller was named an auditor*
*of the 1994 synod in Rome on consecrated life.*

*Grounded in a theology of religious life, this address draws upon both*
*the past and the present to articulate possibilities for the future.*

> Who has seen the wind?
> Neither I nor you:
> But when the leaves hang trembling
> The wind is passing through
> Who has see the wind?
> Neither you nor I:
> But when the trees bow down their heads
> The wind is passing by.[1]

This whimsical lyric by Christina Rossetti reminds us how suscep-
tible we are to the influence of unseen forces. The wind's traces may
be gentle, as in the poet's vision, or fierce. At one moment wind
soothes, shapes, and guides; at another it rips and tears. It rustles
leaves, lifts kites, powers sails, and supports wings. It can also destroy
homes, uproot trees, and down power lines. Invisible but not silent,
wind whispers and sings and sobs and roars. Wind can be fickle or
frightening; it can also be life-giving and renewing.

Anyone who has lived apostolic women's religious life in the
United States in the last thirty years knows what it is to be buffeted
and shaped by powerful but sometimes unseen forces from every side.
Continuing the analogy, we could liken the pressures on us to winds
from the four compass points. From the east came the expectations
of the institutional church, whether Roman or American: conciliar
documents, *Essential Elements*, canonical requirements, diocesan
policies and procedures. These influences helped to launch and vali-
date our renewal, but also created tensions between our own insights
and official mandates and interpretations.

From the south came the winds of liberation theology. The bishops at Medellín and Puebla and our sisters missioned in Latin America sent messages of a new way of being with the poor, of doing theology, of being church.[2]

Our west winds were the forces of our own society and culture. Enjoined by the Second Vatican Council to make our own "the joys and the hopes, the griefs and the anxieties of the people of this age," we adapted our lifestyles and ministries to new needs. At the same time we experienced and adapted to the revolutions in science, technology, communication, transportation, the political and social orders, popular culture and the media which characterized all of Western society.

To the northern point on the compass we can assign the steadying influence of our own founding charisms and sound traditions, newly researched and interpreted for contemporary life.

From north, south, east, and west, then, the winds of change have carried us to this place and shaped our present reality. How can we describe that reality?

In the decades after the Second Vatican Council the winds of change propelled us through some incredibly difficult terrain: misunderstandings without, polarizations within, loss of membership, lack of resources, pastoral disappointments. Along the way we have acquired an unprecedented level of academic and professional preparation for ministry (but we sometimes confuse professional achievement with ministerial effectiveness). We have a spirituality cultivated through individual faith journeys (but we are less sure how to integrate it into a communal experience). We have highly developed skills in group participation (but less skill in calling forth and affirming individual leadership). Overall, compared to twenty years ago, American women religious today are more grounded in charism, more self-aware as women, more appreciative of diversity, more aware of the interdependent causes of social ills, and as committed as ever to alleviating the suffering of the poor, the needy, and the vulnerable.

Moreover, the processes of renewal have freed and empowered us. We have eliminated irrelevant and outmoded symbols and practices. We have grown into new theological, spiritual, educational, psychological insights. So the moment has come to ask, What kind of future can we look forward to? The answer—our future—depends, as it always has, on the mysterious work of God's providence in our regard. But the future also depends, as it always has, on how we answer the depth questions. These are perennial questions which have to be answered in every time and place. The prospect that the upcoming synod may ask and answer these questions strikes fear in some. But there is no reason to fear. These are not questions that can be answered by a synod, or by assemblies or chapters or planning teams, no matter how motivated or sophisticated. The answers to these questions can be borne out of and lived only within the hearts and lives of our members.

There are only a small number of such depth questions, but in light of the theme of these days together, charism and mission, I would like to focus on two of them: the question of our ecclesial identity and of our mission in the postmodern world.[3] The two questions are interrelated as being and action: identity is expressed in mission. Moreover, the four winds of change—messages from the institutional church, from liberation theologies, from our U.S. culture, and from our traditions—have given each question its distinctive form today.

(Before going on, I want to note that I am using the phrase "apostolic religious life" throughout these remarks in an inclusive and nontechnical sense, to distinguish our topic from contemplative religious life rather than from its monastic or evangelical forms.)

## Ecclesial Identity

The question of ecclesial identity can be asked from two perspectives: First, does women's apostolic religious life occupy an essential or unique place in the church? Second, is visible membership and participation in the church critical to the identity of women's apostolic religious life? *How important are we to the church, and how important is membership in the church to us?*

The question of ecclesial identity seen from either perspective would have sounded absurd a few decades ago when the signs of our identification with the church were so distinctive—our dress, dwellings, lifestyles, and ministries signaled that we were a special and esteemed group in the church. The question of identity had been answered along the same lines ever since the founding of most of our congregations. But one of the effects of renewal has been to lay open the question in our new context.[4] First, let's examine it from the perspective of our place in the church.

History shows us that religious life began in the third century when disciples began to gather around the early desert solitaries. But most of our modern apostolic congregations arose after the Reformation, with the greatest number founded in the eighteenth and nineteenth centuries. Clearly, what has not always existed in the church need not always exist. Neither religious life in general nor apostolic religious life in the form in which we know it today is essential to the constitution of the church.

However, the Second Vatican Council affirmed that religious life is inseparable from the life and holiness of the church, an encomium which suggests a distinct identity.[5] What is that identity? Generally, the Dogmatic Constitution on the Church defines us as laypersons in a specific canonical state. I say generally because in one passage it says that laity are "all the faithful except those in holy orders and those in the religious state" (31), thus signaling a fundamental ambiguity: are we laity or not? As we know, a key achievement of the council was to transform our understanding of church from that of a hierarchical institution, a perfect society in which religious occupy a special "state of perfection," into a people of God in which all members are equally called to a life of holiness. That ecclesial vision highlights baptismal consecration and the significance of the lay vocation; it is less clear in affirming any distinct contribution of religious life to the church.

As the years have passed, this theoretical ambiguity has grown in the practical order. How many people really believe that religious life is a gift to the whole Christian community, not just to the men and women who embrace it? What are the consequences of that gift in the lives of the hierarchy, the clergy, other laity, the poor and the marginalized, and those in need? What difference does the presence of apostolic women religious, as a specific group rather than as single individuals, make to the life of a parish, a diocese, or an institution?

It seems to me that the answer to the question of ecclesial identity is that, fundamentally, apostolic women religious are laywomen who have embraced and publicly committed themselves to a distinctive way of following Jesus Christ. Apostolic religious life is a *way of life*, a phrase which connotes a depth and breadth and intensity of commitment far beyond a lifestyle. Lifestyles can be taken up and abandoned by simply changing one's economic status, leisure activities, or diet.

By contrast, a way of life consists of a constellation of fundamental life choices having an internal coherence and consistency. One has *a* way of life, defined by the choices one has made about relationship to God, to the Christian community, to sexuality, to possessions, to companions, to those in need. The way of life known as religious life is a radical response to the call of Jesus who says, "I am the way." By analogy, the early church described itself as "the Way," a commitment to following Christ to which every other choice is subordinated (Acts 9:2). Author Judith Merkle describes religious life as a categorical choice, that is, a choice that eliminates other choices. She notes, "Religious life involves more than social action, professional excellence, or holistic living. Rather, it is a life project built on a relationship."[6] Religious life is a continual call to conversion. It is dynamic, as the fundamental choices deepen and mature and the consequences of those choices are played out in different circumstances. The totality of these choices, lived with visible and passionate commitment, clearly distinguishes us from other laity in the church and offers a unique witness.

I suggest that, in the processes of renewal, our identity has been weakened because we have not tended enough to the internal consistency, the congruence, among the depth choices which define our way of life. Celibacy, prayer, community, mission should all interact and contribute to the fundamental unity at its core. For example, the witness of celibate community is a powerful expression of ministry; ministry engenders passion in prayer; prayer purifies the heart of attachment to material things; renunciation of material things brings us closer to the poor and the needy, etc.

Is it accurate or helpful to describe our way of life as charismatic? Yes and no. On the positive side, this designation highlights the spontaneity, the diversity, the creativity, the gratuity of religious life. The Pauline passages on charism are eloquent and well known. However, it must be noted that they apply to all Christians. All—bishops, clerics, laity, religious—are called and gifted in a variety of ways. Since the council, however, the term has been appropriated by religious to refer to the grace of founding a congregation, to its characteristic spirituality, to its mission, to the gifts and graces of individual members, and to religious life as a way of life. I suggest that the imprecision of the term has greatly diminished its usefulness. The distinctiveness of each congregation might better be identified with its tradition or its deep story.[7] Furthermore, the description of religious life as charismatic sometimes heightens the tension between institutional or hierarchical elements of the church and the charismatic in a way which is not helpful. The reality of the church is much more profound and complex than this simple dichotomy.

Let me move on to the second aspect of the ecclesial identity issue: How significant is public membership and participation in the church to our identity as apostolic women religious? Any of you who have processed a dispensation for a sister who says that she is comfortable being a community member, but no longer feels at home in the Roman Catholic Church, knows what this issue is. Any of you who experience the tension among congregational members over including—or not including—a Eucharistic liturgy within a congregational celebration recognize another aspect of the issue.

If we go back into our congregational histories we recognize that our foremothers sought and prized public identification with the church. Some congregations experienced painful struggles when church officials threatened to withhold recognition that founders regarded as rightfully theirs. More recently, our perseverance through the process of approval of constitutions, despite requirements that were sometimes arbitrary, insensitive, or oppressive, testified that basically we know ourselves to be, and want recognition as, congregations within the Roman Catholic Church.

This desire persists despite the growing pain caused by the transformation of our consciousness as women and our realization that the church itself institutionalizes sexism within and fails to denounce it without. How can we justify this continued commitment to public identification with the church, and what does it call us to?

Our commitment rests on our knowledge that at baptism we were each born again into life in Christ and into that extension of Christ's presence and work throughout space and time known as the church. Within the church we are taught, nourished, forgiven, reconciled. The church is not just a spiritual concept or an individual personal experience. It is a collection of human beings from every race and nation and condition, united by the one Spirit in a visible and public community of disciples.

At religious profession we renewed our baptismal commitment and thus signaled that membership in the church is intrinsic to the way of life we were choosing. The choice for a life in union with Christ is a choice for a life within Christ's church.

Sometimes this is not an easy place to be. We share membership with those who are flawed, confused, limited in many ways. In our more honest moments we recognize flaws and limitations in ourselves. Furthermore, within the church there is a differentiation of roles, responsibilities, and gifts. To paraphrase St. Paul, "Not all are apostles, prophets, teachers, workers of mighty deeds" (1 Cor. 12:29–30). But the greatest gift, the one that is the hallmark of a Christian and the criterion by which all else is judged, is love. It is our love for Christ and for the community united in Christ which impels and sustains our commitment to membership. To allow ourselves to be alienated from the church is to surrender our birthright; it is to deprive ourselves of life-giving nourishment; it is to be exiled from our true home. Furthermore, public estrangement from the church deprives its other members of the witness of our love, our truth, and our fidelity.

To summarize this first part of these reflections then, apostolic religious life is a distinct way of life within the Christian community, characterized by a complex of fundamental choices. Among these choices is the choice for explicit membership in the Catholic Church. Religious congregations, because they exist to facilitate and promote the way of life of their members, also have a public identity within the church.

## The Mission of Apostolic Religious Life

Our second depth question is *What should be the mission of apostolic women's religious life today and in the future?* Our world today is very different from that in which our missions were first articulated. The immigrant poor of the nineteenth century have moved up the economic ladder; many of our traditional works have become public responsibilities; the rest of the laity has expanded their role in ministry. Still, the way of life we have espoused is radically for others. We have made a life-long commitment to mission within the context of our individual congregations. Therefore we need to reexamine and, if necessary, restate our mission for this new time and place. This is a work for each congregation, but I suggest that the mission apostolic women religious are called to today should be integral to our way of life, prophetic, global, and corporate.

### Mission as integral to a way of life

Each of our religious congregations was founded to express some facet of the church's mission. Mission is at the heart of our self-understanding, an expression of our identity. The choice to be "in mission" is part of that constellation of fundamental life choices that constitute our way of life. As self-evident as this seems, the identification of mission with our way of life has been eroded from several sides. For example, David Nygren and Miriam Ukeritis, in their study, *The Future of Religious Orders in the United States* (FORUS), describe the "parochial assimilation" of religious life: religious are regarded as interchangeable parish workers, without any significance attached to their identity as religious.[8] The sense of mission as integral to a way of life has also been weakened as a result of financial pressures: sometimes a "job"—anything that pays an adequate salary—seems like the only possible choice of work. The sense of mission is weakened from still another side when, in the absence of a strong commitment to prayer or community, an individual allows her world to be wholly defined by work. Professional ambition and workaholism can replace zeal for mission.

As apostolic women religious, our mission expresses our identity as laity, as women, and as religious. I use laity here in contrast to the clerical vocation. It is true that many of our members are performing ministries which used to be the responsibility of priests. However, the fact that we are doing them demonstrates that they are expressions of the baptismal vocation, not the priestly vocation. Our congregations do not have two classes of members, lay and clerical; we do not have hierarchy built into our way of life. Our radical equality as baptized Catholics is part of who we are within community, and it makes us one with the overwhelming majority of the church's membership.

Our identification with women and as women animates and shapes our mission. *With* women because we have made ourselves present to other women in their hopes, fears, achievements, and struggles. We understand the needs of people for health care, housing, education, economic justice, political representation, moral guidance, spiritual inspiration from a woman's perspective. *As* women because we bring to ministry our personal gifts of courage, compassion, sensitivity, honed through our own life experience.

Finally, our identity as religious shapes our mission. Individual ministries are expressions of a congregational mission; they are shaped and focused by the congregation's tradition. But beyond that, our public identification with a distinctive way of life is itself a witness, a prophetic statement.

## Mission as prophetic

To describe religious life as prophetic does not necessarily connote dramatic speeches and gestures, although some occasions do call for them. Rather, it connotes a transparency to the divine which is the fruit of a life focused on Jesus and which is the real meaning of prophecy—speaking of God. It is not a matter of individually prophetic persons, but of a way of life which, because it involves the deliberate, daily, and publicly identifiable following of Jesus, is prophetic by its nature.[9]

The notion of being publicly identifiable is a challenging one, given the absence of the former markers of public identity such as habit and proximity to a church and employment in a particular setting. It doesn't mean adopting these outward symbols again. Nor does it necessarily imply being recognized as a religious by every casual observer. On the other hand, it doesn't mean fading into anonymity. It means being recognizable to all who would see, who are interested, or who inquire. It requires a facility in drawing the gaze of the inquirer from ourselves to the Gospel which we proclaim and which animates us.

Prophecy demands inculturation lest the word spoken fall on deaf ears. It leads to diverse expressions of religious life as the word is adapted to differing circumstances. Prophecy requires engagement in the public issues of the day if the Gospel is to speak to contemporary human needs. Prophecy requires that we hold our sponsored institutions accountable for the clarity of their Gospel witness.

## Mission as global

A prophetic mission today will also be global in its perspective and outreach. We know from personal experience and observation how the poverty and suffering in one part of the world have their causes in decisions made in another part, and how the elites of the world conspire to enhance their own positions at the expense of the poor and marginalized. We know that greed, lust for power, racial and ethnic animosity, and rape of the earth and its resources know no boundaries. Women and men religious constitute a worldwide network of communication and potential response to human suffering and exploitation. Many of our congregations transcend national borders. Others have members missioned in some of the most remote corners of the globe. Furthermore, we have organizational ties with religious throughout the world through our own Conference and through the International Union of Superiors General.

What is sometimes lacking is an appreciation of the valuable resource we have in our information about realities around the world and creativity in making effective use of the information. As individual congregations and as a Conference we have responded to new needs and specific crises in Eastern Europe, Liberia, Somalia, Central America, Haiti, Rwanda, and many other places. Can we enlarge our commitment to information sharing, analysis, and coordinated action on behalf of a truly world church?

Even if the mission of one's congregation is focused on a particular local church or geographic region, this potential and imperative for global outreach exists through the Leadership Conference as well as through relationships with other congregations.

## Mission as corporate

Perhaps the most challenging dimension of future mission will be its corporate character. In the FORUS study, Nygren and Ukeritis claim that many individual religious and groups have relinquished the power of corporate witness for a variety of individual commitments in effective but unconnected ministerial positions. "The emphasis on individual ministry, or, at times, simply procuring a position, has eclipsed the symbolism of, and statement previously made by, corporate commitments."[10] The situation of individual ministries is not easily reversed, even if it should be. There are only two ways to do so: either everyone is employed within the same institutional ministry or everyone is committed to the same type of service such as ministry to persons with AIDS or to street children. The first solution is only possible where the congregation controls the institution. The latter solution assumes that the type of social problem being addressed will always exist to the same degree of need. Neither solution takes into account the differing talents, energies, and professional expertise of the members.

A new way to think about corporate mission is needed, one which recognizes the changing social realities, engages and focuses the energies of the members, and expresses the public identity of the congregation. It is a corporate mission that is needed, not necessarily corporate ministries. The twofold test of whether a congregational mission is more than rhetoric is how effectively it shapes each member's choices and how much it contributes to the public perception of the congregation.

## Concluding Reflections

The characteristics of mission outlined here—integral to the way of life of apostolic women religious, prophetic, global, and corporate—will be nuanced by the tradition and fresh inspiration of each congregation. Who are we? What is our hearts' desire? How will we spend our talents and energies? Our ability to answer these depth questions about identity and mission with clarity and conviction has implications for new members, for associates, for affiliates. They deserve to know what we are asking them to invest in and to help shape the future.

The questions are our questions. They belong to us before they belong to church officials or synod participants. It is time to speak and live our truth without compromise.

There is a growing temptation among religious today to believe that our choices are limited. We feel constrained by age, by diminishing numbers, by finances, by professional education, by ecclesial expectations to carry on as we are, without really encountering the depth issues. Let us take a lesson from the successful sailor who makes a friend of the wind: buffeted by contrary breezes, he chooses a tack and sets the sails. With one eye on the compass, the sailor strains forward toward the distant shore. Despite the winds buffeting us, we too can set our direction. Our compass is Christ; our sails are woven of faith and hope, courage and love. We can only face forward. Renewal has often invited us to look backward toward the great persons and events of our past. Now it is time to look forward, to the new leaders and creative deeds in our future. There was no golden age of religious life. There were only women and men, human as we are, who loved God, cared for persons in need, and dared to dream. We are as human, as flawed, and gifted as they were, and still in touch with the dream.

We began this hour by reflecting on the four winds of change which have brought us to this place. Let us end by invoking the wind that comes from another direction, the breath of the Spirit which blows where it wills. Sometimes a zephyr, sometimes a mighty gale— God's Spirit can nudge our timid choices, strengthen our frail resolve, reverse any misdirected course. Before he left us, Jesus promised the apostles that they would receive power when the Holy Spirit would come upon them, and they would be his witnesses to the ends of the earth (Acts 1:8). Later, when their time was fulfilled, they were all in one place together. "Suddenly from up in the sky there came a noise like a strong, driving wind which was heard all through the house where they were seated. All were filled with the Holy Spirit. They all begun to express themselves . . . as the Spirit prompted them" (Acts 2:2–4). Now it is our time. Spirit of God, fill us and send us forth with the power and passion of your Word!

## Notes

1. Christina Rossetti, "Who Has Seen the Wind?" in *The Complete Poems of Christina Rossetti* ed. R. W. Crump (Baton Rouge: Louisiana State University Press, 1986), 42.

2. The Latin American Bishops Conference (CELAM) meeting in Medellín, Colombia, in 1968 marked a turning point in the history of the church, as the bishops applied the teachings of Vatican II to a situation of social injustice and what they called institutionalized violence. Later, at Puebla, Mexico, in 1979, they affirmed the church's preferential option for the poor.

3. Joan Chittister, OSB, names ten critical questions which deal with "the very existence of religious life, its relationship to the Church, its present character, its purpose, its spirituality and its energy" in the *National Catholic Reporter*, February 18, 1994.

4. The significance of this question was highlighted by the FORUS study (Future of Religious Orders in the United States) described by David Nygren, CM, and Miriam D. Ukeritis, CSJ, in *Religious Life Future Project: Executive Summary* (Chicago: University Center for Applied Social Research, 1992), 36: "The most compelling result of the FORUS study indicates that a significant percentage of religious no longer understand their role and function in the Church. This lack of role clarity can result in lowered self-confidence, a sense of futility, greater propensity to leave religious life, and significant anxiety. The younger religious experience the least clarity, and among them, women religious experience less clarity than their male counterparts. . . . For both women and men religious, Vatican II substantially reinforced the role of laity in the Church but did not clarify for religious the unique contribution of their vocation."

5. *Lumen Gentium*, 44.

6. Judith A. Merkle contrasts "lifestyle enclaves" with communities in *Committed by Choice* (Collegeville, MN: Liturgical Press, 1992), 21. In the former, persons share some aspects of their essentially private lives; in the latter, they share their deeper meaning-system or commitment. On the contrast between way of life and lifestyle see also David L. Fleming, SJ, in *Religious Life: Rebirth through Conversion*, ed. Gerald A. Arbuckle, SM, and David L. Fleming, SJ (New York: Alba House, 1990), 23 and 33.

7. Tradition is appropriate because it connotes both preservation and development, content and process. Bernard J. Lee, SM, suggests "deep story," a category of interpretation that comes out of structuralism as a method for interpreting group identity, in "A Socio-Historical Theology of Charism," *Review for Religious* (January–February 1989): 124–35.

8. Nygren and Ukeritis, *Religious Life Futures Project*, 37.

9. Elizabeth A. Johnson observes, "a new combination of ancient elements is beginning to define the essential character of religious life. The emerging understanding of this life is primarily that of persons and communities called to prophetic ministry embedded in a contemplative relationship to God." "Between the Times: Religious Life and the Post-Modern Experience of God," *Review for Religious* 53 (1994): 12.

10. Nygren and Ukeritis, *Religious Life Futures Project*, 35.

# 6

## 1996 National Assembly
### *"The Fierce Urgency of Now"*
### *(Imagining Leadership for a Nonviolent World)*

# "LIFT UP YOUR VOICE
# WITH STRENGTH"

## *Nancy Schreck, OSF*

— Atlanta, August 1996 —

*"Our critical spiritual work as leaders in this time is to tend to these issues: identity, imagination, and the capacity for hope." Nancy Schreck addressed the annual Assembly on the LCWR's fortieth anniversary with a call to demonstrate "a different way to be a society" in the midst of violence at home and abroad.*

*In a brief period of time, NATO troops had entered Sarajevo, Israel's prime minister was assassinated, and more than 150 died in the bombing of a federal building in Oklahoma City. The Bosnian war ended, but peace talks in Northern Ireland begun in the late 1980s struggled toward tenuous agreements punctuated by continued violence. The Taliban moved to take control of Afghanistan, and FBI agents hunted down the Unabomber in the wilderness of Montana. U.S. bankers found increasing attraction in derivative investing. Dolly, the cloned sheep, was born.*

*In Beijing the United Nations convened the Fourth World Conference on Women, and a month later John Paul II addressed the UN General Assembly, the second papal visit following the first and historic visit of Paul VI during Vatican II. The next year John Paul published* Vita Consecrata, *his reflections on religious life and mission drawn from the proceedings of the 1994 Synod. The prison ministry experience of Helen Prejean, CSJ, was transformed from book to film in* Dead Man Walking, *and capital punishment gained new prominence in popular debate.*

*Just prior to the 1996 Assembly, more than four hundred LCWR members stood in prayer at the gates of Fort Benning in Columbus, Georgia, calling for the closure of the School of the Americas (SOA), a training facility for Latin American military personnel linked to human rights abuses in their home countries. A few days later, the LCWR members listened to their president calling them to "the urgency of this moment" and to a vision grounded in imagination and hope.*

With all we have heard these days about the reality of violence in our world, nation, church, and personal lives, I do not really need to remind you that we lead in a time:

- ◆ when urban children in the United States go to bed to the sound of gunfire, and when in 1994, one million children were victims of abuse, a figure that increased 27 percent from just four years previous;

- ◆ when in one year, 1993, the nation spent $3 billion in services for victims of gunshot trauma: many treated in health care facilities sponsored by our congregations, with an average cost for one hospitalized victim of $33,000;[1]

- ◆ when the bonds of family and neighborhood are fraying, and the most violent place in the United States is not our streets, but our homes;

- ◆ when more than half of the women murdered in this country are killed by their partner or ex-partner;[2]

- ◆ when our most basic virtues seem to be deteriorating;

- ◆ when both domestically and globally we are deeply divided along lines of race, class, gender, religion, and culture;

- ◆ when environmental degradation and resource scarcity threaten to explode our divisions into perpetual conflict and when the first means to settling conflict is violence;

- ◆ when nearly all of the press releases by the LCWR this year dealt with violence: Chiapas [Mexico], Dianna Ortiz, the burning of black churches, immigration, just to name a few.[3]

We are leading in a time when an illness of spirit seems to have spread across our land. Violence is all around us, and seeps into us.

What can we do to be peacemakers in this land of violence? The prophet Isaiah said to the people living in another troubled time and says to us, "Lift up your voice with strength" (Isa. 40:9). In other words, say something, do something. Make a response. Take action. For we have much at stake and much to contribute. We have heard enough. It is time to go forth from here to act.

As we leave our National Assembly I suggest two significant actions. The first is to imagine a nonviolent world, to believe from our depths that violence is not our destiny. The second is to lead our congregations to corporate action which changes the world in which we live.

When we imagine a nonviolent world we will experience ourselves as exiles in a culture of violence. This is not a new experience in the faith. Our ancestors, from biblical times until the founding of our congregations and beyond, often experienced their values to be utterly at odds with those of the dominant culture. The prophets encouraged people to believe during these difficult times and to uphold their vision so radically in tension with the world in which they lived. They gave this encouragement because the prophets knew that the experience of exile was extremely difficult and required a kind of faith that easier times did not demand. In order to survive in exile the people needed to maintain three things: their identity, their imagination, and their capacity for hope. Our critical spiritual work as leaders in this time is to tend to these issues: identity, imagination, and the capacity for hope.

## Identity

Our first work is to foster members' sense of their identity as exiles whose values are clearly at odds with those of the dominant culture. Exiles need to be at home in their minority status, which means having a certain tolerance for being misunderstood, living without the respect we all desire, and acting in ways that many perceive as meaningless or threatening. It means, as *Vita Consecrata* states, choosing community in a culture of isolation and individualism, having a passion for mission in which the goal is service not status, and living prophetically. This is difficult work because many of our members find the respect of their companions, the affirmation of civic and church leaders to be a significant value they hesitate to sacrifice for exilic identity.

## Imagination

One of the things we learn from biblical exile is that Babylon wanted to capture not only the bodies of the Israelite people but their imagination. This was necessary because as long as Israel maintained its imagination, its vision of life, its courage, then the empire would be unstable and provisional. It was critical that the exiles not allow their spirit to be domesticated, not an easy task in a hostile environment. Our second work is to keep imagination alive, to support our members in their ability to hold and practice faith in an empire that is deeply hostile to our most precious social vision, to keep our congregations from being domesticated. Essential in this process for the biblical exiles was the grounding of their life and vision in the fidelity of God, which endures and will sustain in every circumstance. It is our role then, to speak not only of activism but also of the power and purpose of God who "does not faint or grow weary," "who gives power to the faint, and strengthens the powerless" (Isa. 40:28–30). What these and so many related passages indicate is that this dream of a nonviolent world is not something of our own making, but is a cosmic commitment that originates in the very heart of God. One of our critical tasks as leaders is to remember this commitment made by God. It is a commitment deeper than our actions, outlasting our resolve, and withstanding any assault of the empire. On this we can rest our lives. It is God's deep and abiding commitment to peace that calls us to peacemaking. The ideology of the dominant culture cannot stop the movement toward peace. This conviction is our ultimate safeguard against cynicism, conformity, and despair.

How can we sustain this imaginative view? Again, the answer I would like to explore comes from the biblical tradition.[4] Exiles are sustained in their alternative passion with power and freedom gained from the regular practice of intentional and alternative liturgy, which must be understood in its biblical sense. Liturgy for the exile is the regular communal process of looking at life and experience through an alternative set of metaphors, symbols, stories, and hopes that the community takes to be normative and nonnegotiable. When we process our experience through memories of exodus, exile, crucifixion, resurrection, we see life differently. What fatigued peacemaking exiles most need is to have life mediated in fresh ways alternative to the story created by television news. When we do not have alternative stories we become dull and our spirits suffer. What we need is for our imaginations to be fed by stories of Esther courageously standing before the king intervening on behalf of her people, of Judith risking her life to protect her nation. We need stories of Elizabeth never giving up hope that life can come from barrenness, and of Mary Magdalene, disbelieved by the disciples, who became the "apostle to the apostles." We need to hear Jesus' invitation to share in free healing and to eat at a table where no one is excluded. We need to be in the places where we hear stories from women who have broken the cycle of abuse, stories of people who have learned ways to treat the land with respect, stories of neighbors who have bonded to reduce gang violence. Such accounts stun the empire and give freedom, hope, courage to the listening community. We need this vision because after awhile we are spent and dry, and we cannot generate any more action. So, if we are to imagine a nonviolent world we must let ourselves hear that justice and nonviolence are deep resolves of God, and God's people can act to bring them about.

## Hope

Like the Israelite people seeking to live an alternative vision, we need to gather to articulate our fear, hurt, doubt, and anger. We need to gather to practice lament, to publicly express those things that diminish, dehumanize, immobilize. We must dare to express our pain that the world in which we live is not holding sacred the view of its maker. Israel did not pretend that the empire was an acceptable home, or that the experience of violence and oppression was natural or bearable. It said a bold, pathos-filled "No" to the circumstances of life. In the biblical view it is necessary that exiles speak in raw, dangerous, honest ways that "settled people" never find necessary or permissible. The miracle is that in biblical liturgy, despair is not the last word. There is always a movement to hope, joy, and rescue given by the Holy One who comes decisively and transformatively into the situation of hurt and loss. Only after proclaiming hurt can the people hear God speaking assurances that changes would come. "Lift up your voice in strength, say to the cities of Judah, behold your God" (Isa. 49:9).

To put all that in other words, tell everyone you know that the God of justice has overcome all power of injustice. The giver of *shalom* has nullified all perpetrators of violence and death. So believe, and sing, and dance. Freedom, mercy, peace are decreed by God. This is the radical alternative to violence that we claim. Surely the powers still rage, but we are people with imagination, and we will not slip into despair nor yield the vision that guides us.

All this is about liberating our imagination, about doing what is necessary not to think like the world thinks. It is our role as spiritual leaders to foster this alternative imagination; to make time for honest talk about the fears, hurts, and hopes in the struggle for a different world view; to tell each other stories that encourage radical action; and to foster deep hope in the One who is beyond all our work. As leaders we need to provide a place for risking imaginative transformation because serious energy for peacemaking never comes from the normative and authorized stories of those in power. As Audre

Lorde says, "The master's tools will never dismantle the master's house."[5] Identity, imagination, and courageous hope are encouraged by alternative stories, evoked by bearing witness to a God known by the exiles of the dominant culture, those tilted toward marginality. They are mediated through the raw reality of social pain. Only through such experience can we imagine something other than we know now, can we dream of peace, have the power to act on our dreams, gain the courage to embrace and trust this other way of life, to act, risk, believe, and hope relentlessly against the odds.

Walter Brueggemann says that "peacemaking requires a kind of freedom that comes from the imaginative disengagement from the visible power arrangements around us and the imaginative embrace of another scenario of the world rooted in another voice, based in another memory, authorized toward another humanity."[6]

So our first work as leaders is the spiritual work of grounding ourselves in the imaginative reality that a world without violence is possible.

Our second action is to go from this place imagining ourselves as the leaders our congregations need to make a difference in the world in which we live. This does not mean creating some sort of elitist, messiah complex. It does mean developing the skills necessary to move our congregations to continued and deepened influence on the world in which we live.

Imagine yourself as a leader with vision and clarity regarding the mission of your congregation. See yourself as someone who can not only take direction from the group but can also set direction that others will recognize as good. Be willing to do the disciplined work of self-reflection, study, and contemplation, as well as group discernment so that you can be clear about what is critical for your time in leadership. As a leader know that it is your role to keep the mission in focus, no matter how frenzied things become or how great the pressures to compromise. Imagine yourself as a leader who can make the mission of the congregation come alive in the hearts and minds of your members.

A great challenge for leadership in this regard is to move our members to embrace a common mission, with group goals and commitments. It is our task to develop ways to engage the common energy and vision of the group, to mesh individual efforts in the realization of a corporate mission. This is not an easy task. First of all, many of our members are doing fine things in their individual efforts. Second, it involves making efforts to address the apathy, disengagement, and self-absorption of some of our members. Now I am not advocating "group think" here. But I believe that if we want to impact our church and society, we need the power of many talented women moving in the same direction. As you well know from *A Critical Juncture* (the viability study of religious congregations), this sense of mission is a critical indicator of viability.

It is my belief that real leadership is reflected in the inspired actions of others. We traditionally have assessed leaders personally. But perhaps we should assess leadership by the degree to which people around the leaders are inspired. When a group of people is empowered, energized, open, creative, when the group shares a mission, the synergy that develops allows them to accomplish almost anything.

Imagine yourself as a pioneer leader, one willing to venture into unknown territory with only the most primitive map and guide your congregation into new and unfamiliar destinations demanded by the critical needs of our time. As a pioneer leader you dream the great dreams about the elimination of violence in all its forms: hunger, poverty, racism, sexism, and any kind of oppression. You find ways to mobilize your group to corporate action in that delicate dance of both initiating new ministries and supporting existing institutional ministries struggling to respond to these new needs.

It is not always easy even for the best minds to predict the choices that are most critical for the future. In 1905 Grover Cleveland said that "Sensible women do not want to vote." In 1920, Robert Millikan, the Nobel Prize winner in physics, said "There is no likelihood that man [humans] can ever tap the power of the atom." Simon Newcomb was an astronomer of some note when in 1902 he predicted, "Flight by machines heavier than air is unpractical and insignificant, if not utterly impossible." In 1943, Thomas Watson, chairman of IBM at the time, said "I think that there is a world market for about five computers." In 1977, Ken Olsen, president of Digital Equipment, said, "There is no reason for any individual to have a computer in their home."[7]

I realize that all the examples I have used are from men, and I would like to have added some from women but I was unable to find any. I will leave it to you to decide whether such statements have, like so much of our history, not been recorded, or if women have never made such poor predictions.

If we are going to be able to lead well, we must be able to go where there is no well-worn path. We will have to be bold women who will help our groups dream new dreams about how to live the Gospel in this time. We will need courage to bring these dreams to life. Imagine yourself as a leader willing to take risks, be daring, and to learn by your mistakes. Model this and I believe you will create this spirit in your congregation.

I know I am not talking about something easy. We all know that risk usually creates resistance. We need to be leaders able to stand up to those survival and comfort urges that loom so large in the individual and group psyche. In the face of our basic survival needs, we need to be able to step out in faith and say that we are not about the preservation of an institution but about participating in God's transforming purposes. Key here is foreseeing the unforeseeable and having the courage to act on that knowledge or hunch.

To lead in this way we need the contemplative activity of knowing clearly both our fears and our source of courage. Fear has the potential of extinguishing leadership, but it only becomes a problem when permitted to run rampant through our lives, unacknowledged, unnamed, untamed, and unembraced. Courage on the other hand ignites leadership. It resists self-serving justifications, it sparks energy, it invites common exploration of the future, it challenges us to search for a common good. Courage involves knowing the dangers that face us and acting anyway. Harriet Tubman knew the risks of helping escaped slaves and acted anyway. Courage is what gives us the power to withstand the pain of difficult times. It acknowledges, embraces, and transforms our fears. It propels us beyond out comfort zones, to act on what is worthy of our commitment.

Now imagine yourself as a leader who is undaunted by our diminishment, who never uses size or age or lack of resources to excuse yourself or your congregation from action. For though we are at a time when our age and numbers tempt us to think small, we are called to think big.[8] See yourself as a leader who can use what you have. Remember the time there were five thousand hungry people gathered on a hillside. Jesus said to the disciples, "You give them something to eat," as if it were the simplest thing in the world. And you know how the story goes—together they did it. The lesson is that when we are faced with seemingly impossible odds, it is important to use what we have, and it will prove to be enough. In every crisis, we have at hand the resources for some means of response if we will open our eyes to see. Biblical parables abound with stories of the inconspicuous beginnings of new realities: a few seeds in the soil, only a little leaven in the bread, a mustard seed. Faith always begins at the point of powerlessness.

We are also learning from modern science that the old notion that only massive amounts of energy can produce large-scale change is crumbling. We are discovering triggering mechanisms in cybernetics and miniaturization in computers. These things demonstrate that small units of energy can affect the largest systems. This is a concept that has yet to affect the way we see the world. We still equate largeness with power. Smallness can be virtue. How paradoxical, how counter to all our fantasies. When God seeks to turn the world around, one person is often enough! I am not crazy. Of course there is room for massive movements and I would love to see some, but I want to remove our excuses of identifying ourselves as too small or insignificant to make a difference.

In "The Shut-In Freedom Fighter," Hope Harle-Mould shares a true story of the power of one woman. This older woman in the midst of failing health, dedicates her isolation, time, and energy to writing letters for the freeing of prisoners of conscience. Through Amnesty International she adopts an unjustly detained political prisoner in Indonesia. The organization gave her sole responsibility for obtaining his release from prison. She knows little about the case at first, but writes letter after letter to the prisoner's family, as well as countless impassioned pleas to every governmental official in Indonesia, from the country's dictator to the guards at her prisoner's jail. After many months and hundreds of letters, she receives a letter from her prisoner, who is finally free.

The letter reads:

> They kept seeing and hearing my name. I was lost. I was nothing to them. Thank God for you, my woman. You kept my name alive. When they finally released me, they said my file was two inches thick with correspondence. Most of it was from you. They said the file was too much trouble for just one prisoner. I owe you my life. Words can never express my thanks. May every political prisoner's file become two inches thick.

Now she could die in peace, knowing that she had saved one person. "Except for one thing, that last thing he had said . . . even yet she types."[9]

Too often churches, social change organizations, and our congregations misguidedly think of effectiveness solely in terms of numbers—if we were larger we would be able to make a difference. But if we were to perform an analysis of origins of movements we would discover that almost every change in the world can be traced to a few people or even one individual determined to make a difference. France was forced to stop nuclear testing in the Pacific by one woman—Helen Caldicott. The campaign for an international code governing the marketing of infant formula was largely the work of three people: Leah Marguiles, Mark Ritchie, and Douglas Johnson. The credit for discovering the circle of poison created by the export of U.S.-banned pesticides to poor countries goes not to scientists of agricultural colleges, not to watchdogs in the government, but to a solitary Peace Corps worker in Afghanistan, David Weir, who noticed that Kool-Aid sold there contained cyclamates, even though they were banned in the United States. These are but pebbles from the mountain of stories of plain people moved to action. Think about the impact we could have if, for example, each of our congregations exerted whatever influence we had to implement the United Nations "Platform for Action" from the Beijing Conference.

I am not naïve. I know that usually the small is crushed, the powerless lose, truth seems forever on the scaffold and wrong forever on the throne, dreams of success fade and are abandoned in despair. But it is my belief that we have here in this room an ability to change the world. I have this audacious hope that each action we take, no matter how small, not only sandbags the levee against the flood of human evil, but inspires others to lend their effort to this work. My hope does not reside only in confidence in our capacities, it is grounded in God, who creates out of nothing and who has chosen "things lowly to overthrow the existing order" (1 Cor. 1:28).

We get what we focus on. When you look at your congregation what do you see—the obstacles or the opportunities? We have a choice. Too often we lose our best energy because we are so focused on the reasons we can't attain something that we have little energy available to focus on what needs to be done to get where we want to be.

In April 1978, when he was seventy-three, Karl Wallenda, patriarch of one of history's greatest tight-rope walking families, was going to walk a high wire between two hotels in San Juan, Puerto Rico. The rope would be 120 feet high. Halfway across Karl lost his balance, plunged to the ground, and died. Afterwards his wife said that all Karl thought about for three months prior to the walk was falling. This was the first time in his life he ever focused this way. What happened, she said, "is that he put all his energy into not falling rather than walking the tightrope."

Imagine yourself as a leader who fosters the intellectual formation of your members so that they will be prepared to do the analysis necessary to respond to complex situations in today's world. Teach your members that if we are to confront the violence in our world we must be able to do social analysis that stands up under the greatest scrutiny the dominant culture will provide. Develop skills whereby your members will be systems thinkers, for violence is not merely an activity, it is a system. It is supported by economic and political assumptions and by structures that drive us toward conflict that is often resolved with violence in subtle or direct forms. These systems and assumptions are deeply embedded, and many times they are difficult to discern, but it is these very assumptions and institutions that we must question. Be a leader who knows that naïveté in this regard is not a virtue.

A story in the *Des Moines Register* (June 23, 1996) will demonstrate the significance of this need. The Sisters United News, representing congregations in Iowa and southwest Wisconsin, placed an ad in the newspaper calling for the closure of the School of the Americas. In the same edition of the paper was an article about the ad including a response from Major Gordon Martel, a spokesman for the School of the Americas. The major said, "The Sisters are well intentioned but are misinformed and wrong." He went on to explain that the program included peacemaking, leadership training to counter narcotics, and a strong component of human rights training" *The Sisters are well intentioned but misinformed and wrong!* How do we counter such patronizing attitudes? By knowing what we are talking about. By being well informed and clear about the issues. As leaders we need to promote an environment of intelligent analysis of information among our members. I do not mean overwhelming them with facts and figures which tend to paralyze, not empower people. Rather it is essential to know the membership well enough to know what it needs, to provide opportunities for both intellectual and experiential learning, skill development, and then invitation to action.

Imagine yourself as a leader who is able to speak credibly about violence because you have been there. Many of us have. We have come from violent homes, experienced sexual, physical, and emotional abuse. Some of us have served in El Salvador, Burundi, or other war-torn places. Some have lived in the inner city or in regions of rural poverty with the violence that brings. But many of us, especially now that we are in leadership, grow removed from this world to which we want to speak. And nothing rings more hollow than pious statements about confronting violence in a nonviolent way from those who sit securely in their offices, isolated from the world in which so many of our sisters and brothers live. Oh, we know stories of violence, but from the newspaper, not from the woman who lives next door afraid to leave her home after dark. If our call for nonviolence is to be more than a musing of the upper-class comfortable ones, we must be where our words take us.

If we are to be credible we must also find ways to support the healing and recovery of our sisters because so many of us have been badly wounded by forces of hatred, misogyny, racist fears, homophobia, and other forms of violence and abuse. We must tend to the dismantling of any structures in our congregations that subject our members to continuing violence.

Imagine yourself as a woman leader in the public arena. This ability takes a special skill that may not be well developed in many women. Much of our social conditioning and leadership development has been stereotypically oriented to the private sphere with needed skills of nurture.[10] What is of concern here is that while this may help us with leadership for the inner life of the congregation, it does little to assist us with our public roles and our place in creating a nonviolent world. The difficulty is that too often when we come to the public sphere of leadership for social impact, we come with the skills useful in the private sphere. The social justice agenda requires a leader able to be in the public eye, willing to stir up conflict for the sake of justice, to be assertive when necessary, able to show appropriate righteous anger, to take initiative, and to organize actions within and on behalf of the community. These are the skills we must exercise if we expect our groups to make an impact. In earlier times we were able to impact by sheer numbers; now we have to use alternative methods. Many of us are more comfortable as nurturers, but that may be a very dangerous approach in these days when the needs of the world make great demands on us. It is a difficult task to form our-selves and our members for public ministry. I challenge us to develop methods of mentoring and supporting each other in this more public leadership.

Finally, imagine yourself as a leader who has created a few ene-mies because you stand for something. See yourself as a woman who is able to exert plenty of moral indignation so that things will not stay the way they are. Gustavo Gutiérrez says, "The Gospel does not tell us not to have enemies—it tells us to love our enemies, to see them as our sisters and brothers." Zora Neale Hurston, in *Dust Tracks on the Road*, looks over her life and says, "I have served and been served. I have made some good enemies for which I am not a bit sorry. I have loved unselfishly." I say this not because I believe in people being enemies, but as Thomas Long from Princeton says, "The most powerful form of communication is still one human being standing up and speaking courageous truth."[11] If we do so, we are bound to find enemies that we must learn how to love.

*"The Fierce Urgency of Now: Imagining Leadership for a Nonviolent World."* Be leaders with a sense of the fierce urgency of now! I invite you to go forth from this place knowing that now is a critical time. I do not care if you have one year left on your tenth term or are in the first month of your first term. Now is the time. When Esther began to see the reality of her ability to influence the well-being of the Jew-ish people, Mordecai reminded her, "perhaps it is for this time that you were born, who knows? Perhaps you have come to royal dignity for just such a time as this," and Esther acted to set her people free (Esther 4:14). Perhaps it was for this time of leadership for a nonvio-lent world that you were born!

Dr. King in his now famous "I Have a Dream" speech[12] reminded us of the critical importance of acting in our time in history. He said,

> We have come to this hallowed spot to remind America of the fierce urgency of now.

> This is no time to engage in the luxury of cooling off or to take the tranquilizing drug of gradualism.

Now is the time to make real the promise of democracy.

Now is the time to rise from the dark and desolate valley of segregation to the sunlit path of peace and racial justice.

Now is the time to lift our nation from the quicksand of racial injustice to the solid rock of brotherhood.

Now is the time to make justice a reality for all God's children.

*It would be fatal to overlook the urgency of this moment.* Sisters, for too long we served as chaplains to society and tended to accommodate and reflect our culture rather than challenge it. We blessed America's individualism, its economic and political systems, and we practiced the violence of its racism and other forms of elitism. Now we need to be contrast communities, avoiding cultural accommodation, demonstrating a different way to be a society. All this must not be left up to chance, and you are in a position to do something about it.

These are difficult times. They call for courageous leaders with great imagination. Surely we will meet with failure and discouragement, but I challenge us to embrace the challenges that face us as steps on the road to wisdom.

Denise Shekerjian studied forty winners of the MacArthur Award. She concluded that the great ideas of these artists, scientists, and social movers and shakers were born of a combination of instinct and judgment. She says, "What intuition provides is an inkling, an itch, a yearning, a mist of possibilities. What judgment provides is structure, assessment, form, purpose."[13] Blending them together with a strong dose of moral imagination will lead to opportunities that, if pursued, may well be a dramatic flowering of the most creative work of your life.

As we close this Assembly I pray for you.

> A leader's vision
> which is part foresight and part insight,
> full of imagination,
> has a sprinkling of intuition, judgment,

compassion, and good humor,
and includes a healthy dose of drive and passion.

A vision which is well informed,
prepared by a lifetime of learning and experience,
and is able to give attention
to the trends and developments in society.

I pray for your creativity rooted in
the reality of charism of your congregation,
an ability to draw together
the fruit of analysis and contemplation,
some grace for being comfortable with ambiguity,
openness to complexity you cannot fully comprehend
and uncertainties you cannot control,
and, finally, the courage to ask the right questions,
and many of them,
that will lead your congregation
to radical action for nonviolence.

## Notes

1. "Violence in Society," *Health Progress* (March–April 1996): 3.

2. *Confronting a Culture of Violence: A Catholic Framework for Action; A Pastoral Message of the Catholic Bishops* (1994), 3.

3. Dianna Ortiz, an American Ursuline Sister, was abducted and tortured while working in Guatemala. Back in the United States she waged a campaign, including a vigil in front of the White House, to uncover the truth about her experience, and the possible involvement of U.S. agents.

4. Walter Brueggemann, *Interpretation and Obedience: From Faithful Reading to Faithful Living* (Minneapolis: Fortress, 1993), 209.

5. Audre Lorde, *Sister Outsider* (Trumansburg, NY: Crossing Press, 1984), 110.

6. Brueggemann, *Interpretation and Obedience*, 217.

7. Joel A. Barker, *Future Edge: Discovering the New Paradigms of Success* (New York: William Morrow, 1992).

8. Global Education Associates, *Newsletter to Religious Orders* (January 1996): 1.

9. Walter Wink, "The Power of the Small," *Bread for the World* (Fall 1995).

10. Marjorie Bayes and Peter Newton, "Women in Authority: A Social Psychological Analysis (New Haven, CT: Department of Psychiatry, Yale University Medical School, 1977), 3–22.

11. Thomas Long, *Newsweek*, March 4, 1996.

12. James Washington, ed., *A Testament of Hope: The Essential Writings of Martin Luther King Jr.* (San Francisco: Harper & Row, 1986), 218.

13. Denise Shekerjian, *Uncommon Genius* (New York: Viking, 1990), 170.

# 7

## 2003 National Assembly
## "Tending the Holy"

# TENDING THE HOLY THROUGH THE POWER OF SISTERHOOD

## *Mary Ann Zollmann, BVM*

— Detroit, August 22, 2003 —

*In less than a decade, the world had changed irrevocably. As LCWR members listened to Mary Ann Zollmann at the 2003 Assembly, the moment reflected unprecedented challenges and unambiguous terrors in a world that no longer seemed to play by any rules. Yet the message, in sharp contrast to the chaos of the times, called for a power that nurtured rather than destroyed, healed rather than wounded, liberated rather than bound.*

*These were the years of 9/11, the "Axis of Evil," "weapons of mass destruction," and "Shock and Awe." Beyond Iraq and the deposition of its leader, warfare raged between Albanians and Serbs in Kosovo, and between Hamas and Israel in Gaza. Conflict focused on land and resources as Israeli settlements encroached deeper into the occupied Palestinian territories, and starvation and genocide stalked tens of thousands in Darfur. Two teenagers opened fire at their school in Colorado, activists bombed abortion clinics, and a physician was convicted of murder for assisting in a case of voluntary euthanasia. Bill Clinton was acquitted after impeachment hearings, and the controversy surrounding the subsequent presidential election of George W. Bush was resolved by the U.S. Supreme Court. Two years after Britain returned Hong Kong to mainland China, the United States returned the Panama Canal to Panama. The Kyoto agreements to slow climate change came too late for the breakup of ice shelves in the Antarctic. Breakthrough science mapped the human genome, and letters containing anthrax were mailed to U.S. congressional offices.*

*Pedophilia scandals erupted in the church in Boston, soon to be followed by similar revelations in other dioceses. The U.S. bishops' pastoral letter,* Always Our Children, *urged acceptance of gay family members, while Dignity U.S.A. asked for respect and justice for lesbian, gay, bisexual, and transgendered persons. Asian bishops pleaded with Rome for sensitivity to the traditions of Eastern religions; Lutherans and Catholics ended centuries of doctrinal disagreement on faith and salvation. John Paul II discussed religious freedom with Fidel Castro. Dorothy Day became a candidate for canonization. The LCWR collaborated with congregations of men religious to open the Center for the Study of Religious Life at Catholic Theological Union in Chicago and began conversations with women throughout the United States on their role in church and society. Along the way, a weary world took time out to celebrate the new millennium.*

*This address offered LCWR members a perspective on the events of these years through the contours of both symbol and story.*

## The Wisdom of the Basswood Tree: Attend to the Soul-stirring Stories

The seasons of the year have come full cycle since we last gathered as an LCWR Conference. In fall, brilliant gold leaves were superimposed on stories of clerical sexual abuse and hierarchical cover-up. My heart ached for a new creation. In winter, white landscapes soft with peace were superimposed on scenes of Bethlehem streets deserted under Israeli military curfew. My heart ached for salvation. In spring, yellow daffodils were superimposed on faces of Iraqi mothers holding wounded children. My heart ached for resurrection. Once again it is summer. We gather holding this year so tenderly that it hurts. We gather aching for creation, salvation, and resurrection.

Open to the revelation of any words capable of articulating our story as women religious in this year that seems to elude any language at all, I went, in the spirit of this Assembly, to the earth. As I sat near an ancient basswood tree, its massive trunk felled and split open in a storm, I listened for the wisdom pouring forth so liberally from her earthy cavity. She insisted on returning me to three stories that have found a home in my heart this year.

The first is a story I read on the plane on my first trip to Rome for our LCWR annual visitation. On an ordinary day in Lorena Province, Iran, a sixteen-month-old child wanders away from the watchful eye of his babysitter. Three days later the desperate search party enters a cave in the distant mountainside. "They see the dark, round shape of a thick-furred, quiescent she-bear lying against the wall. And then they see the child. He was alive, unscarred, and perfectly well after three days—and well fed, smelling of milk. The bear was nursing the child." Reflecting on this story as she tells it, Barbara Kingsolver writes, "The story of the child and the bear came to me on the same day that I read the year's opening words on the bombing campaign in Afghanistan. I cleaved hard to this story. People not altogether far away from Kabul had been visited by an impossible act of grace. In a world whose wells of kindness seem everywhere to be running dry, a bear nursed a lost child."[1]

The second story found me in one of those contemplative spaces to which we as the LCWR have committed ourselves. It is a story of trees told by Megan McKenna. A tree, hollowed out by another tree that had fallen against it, shelters a fox. As the tree aged, the tree began to wonder what the fox would do for a home when it fell. There was a fragile tree next to this old tree; it wasn't suited to housing anyone and could hardly stand by itself. "The older tree said to the younger one, 'Why don't I just shift a bit and start growing among your roots. It will strengthen your base, and still leave the fox a place to live for a long time to come.' The young tree crept over and the old tree leaned to accommodate its nearness to its insides, and the fox was happy, too. If you listen, you'll hear in the silent woods the secret of the trees: Leaning can make you live forever and your weakest places can be someone else's home."[2]

I came upon the third story as I was searching the LCWR leadership manual, *Leading from Within*, for some resources to guide us during our February National Board meeting. The story, "Awaiting the Dance," by Arthur Boers, is about Karen Ridd and Marcela Rodriguez, arrested by the National Guard in El Salvador. Karen was interrogated and released. However, she refused to leave if Marcela was not released as well. When asked why she would not leave, Karen answered, "Soldiers should understand camaraderie." After a pause, they said, "Yes, we do understand." They put her in the hall with Marcela and removed her handcuffs. The two women clung to each other. Then the unexpected happened. "People kept coming to see us, saying things like, 'Where are the two inseparables?' They didn't say this with the tone of mockery that had been going on all day, but with respect and admiration, and maybe with a bit of awe. I think it was for the strength of human friendship that can surmount what seems to be insurmountable obstacles." Shortly after, they were released.[3]

I stay with these stories that will not let me go. They respond to the ache in my heart: the story of the bear and the child feels like new creation; the story of the trees and the fox feels like salvation; the story of the two women friends and the prison guards feels like resurrection. These stories feel like us.

Where is the resonance between our story as women religious and these stories of bears nursing children, leaning trees providing shelter, and embracing women confounding prison guards? As these stories, ostensibly idealistic, even whimsical, weave their way into my experience of us in the LCWR, they reveal our power as women religious in all its prophetic radicality. In this year, when we have experienced our powerlessness to prevent the war in Iraq or to effect any tangible transformation of abusive systems in our church, power has been at work in us. Countercultural, mutual, relational, it is the authentic power integral to the transformation of our church and of our world. It is the power of sisterhood. In the words of Clarissa Pinkola Estés,

We were made for these times. Ours is a time of almost daily astonishment and righteous rage over the latest degrada-tions of what matters most to civilized, visionary people. The luster and hubris some have aspired to while endors-ing acts so heinous against children, elders, everyday people, the poor, the unguarded, the helpless, is breathtaking. Yet, I urge you to please not spend your spirit by bewailing these difficult times. Especially do not lose hope. The fact is we were made for these times. For years we have been learning, practicing, been in training for and just waiting to meet on this exact plain of engagement.[4]

In our time together this morning I invite us to let a bear and a child, trees, and two women illumine our experience as women reli-gious this year bringing to light the breathtaking gift and responsibil-ity of our shared power. It is my hope that this reflection will be both the cause of sincere celebration and a call to live with even greater courage the revisioned story of creation, salvation, and resurrection that we are.

### A Mother Bear Nurses a Child: Claiming the Communal Power of Creation in the Cave of Contemplation

On the same calendar day two very different stories are breathed into our universe: a bear nurses a child in a cave; the United States bombs Afghanistan. The same calendar day unleashes two opposing powers: the power of utter tenderness; the power of sheer domination. The juxtaposition of these two stories suggests that, integral to claiming the power of tenderness is the experience of being lost. We women religious know what it means to be lost. We know how it feels to be carried away to places of consciousness we would rather not go and may even fear.

As women of the church, we are naming, owning, and addressing our impasse with the hierarchical and patriarchal structures of our church. We are living with the gnawing possibility that our church hierarchy as a whole may not acknowledge the abuse of ecclesial power and so may not engage in the single act of radical transparency integral to dismantling the abusive structures of our church. And we are finding ourselves stirred and shaken to the depths of our own souls as we receive and respond to allegations of misconduct on the part of our members.

As women who are citizens of the United States, we are experiencing pervasive shame, anger, and sadness as we live daily with the arrogance of our U.S. government. Scenes of devastation in Iraq inhabit our souls, the lack of any postwar rehabilitation plans baffle our minds, and the betrayal by our leadership in communicating false intelligence information becomes more than we can absorb. And, in it all, we find ourselves haunted by our own complicity in national and global violence.

In the words of our LCWR statements, "we are saddened; we weep; we are filled with fear; we feel isolated and alone; we feel disheartened and powerless." In the imagery of our story of the child and the bear, we feel lost. And, significantly, like this story, our loss has carried us to the dark cave of contemplation. For three years now, we have renewed our commitment to that cave. We have said over and over to ourselves, to the people of God, to our bishops, to officials around tables in Roman offices, to our president, our secretary of state, our Congress:

> God's dream of unity for our world and for our church can come in our time, only if we are willing to change. It is God's love that will bring conversion and healing to us and through us to the world. We want to enter into contemplation and stir our God-given creativity so as to imagine new ways of responding in love.

In the cave of contemplation we, like the lost child in our story, are being held by a new kind of power, the power of the bear nursing the child. In the cave our Mother-God holds us at her breast. In a radical act of tender mutuality and communion, she pours into us her milk, empowering us to be, like her, bearers of this same countercultural creative power. This power subverts, inverts, dismantles, and converts the power of patriarchy operative in both our church and our world. In the words of Dorothee Soelle,

> Omnipotence and mysticism are mutually exclusive. We shall understand the divine power of creation correctly when we detach it from the images of patriarchal power to command and experience it as the life-energy that shares itself. As its language, prayer brings the unity that is given with creation into awareness. The way we are, we are members of each other. All of us. Everything.[5]

In the cave of contemplation we are found by and refounded in the indissoluble communion of original creation. We experience ourselves as daughters of the mother bear and claim the power of our sisterhood. The fruits of our time in the cave of our communal contemplation are alive in us.

◆ This prayer is alive in one of our recent "Resolutions to Action," which calls us to examine how we use our own power as leaders within our congregations. The authenticity of our challenge to political and religious leaders to use their power humbly rather than arrogantly depends upon our own move from dominating power to the power of friendship in mutual service.

◆ This prayer is alive in our "Public Statement Concerning Sexual Abuse." We grieve with victim-survivors; we stand in solidarity with those who have been falsely accused; we are called to justice, mercy, and forgiveness. In a compassion that extends to victim, those accused, and the perpetrators, we acknowledge that we know ourselves as sisters to them all.

◆ This prayer is alive in the communal voice we as a Conference speak for peace. In a statement issued on the first day of our country's preemptive strike against Iraq, we ground our words in our "deep belief that each person is made in the image of God." Our solidarity is experienced as so intimate that "to do harm to another diminishes us as persons and this act of aggression violates our national soul."

This is the creation story we are telling and it is the only story viable for the ongoing genesis of our church, our world, our earth, our cosmos. Dismantling ecclesial and political patriarchy and hierarchy, it places us humbly and powerfully in the cave where the bear nursing the child makes it possible for our church and our world to be "visited by an impossible act of grace."

### Two Trees Leaning Make a Home for the Other: Claiming the Healing Power of Salvation in the Wild Space of Homelessness

I sit with the second story, that of the two trees leaning toward one another to make a home for the fox. I am stirred by the older tree bent on empowering the more fragile tree to collaborate in the creation of a home, even to the cost of her life. How did the older tree get to be this way? And why is this story so captivating me right now? Perhaps the entry point of response to both of those questions lies in the first line of the story, "A tree, hollowed out by another tree that had fallen against it, shelters a fox." The tree itself has been hollowed out, emptied out, has suffered in a way that moves her to make and to be a home. Does this intense yearning to create a home for others come from our own experienced homelessness? This question evoked two experiences I have had this year as LCWR president, experiences that have hollowed me out in a suffering I can only name as a deep sense of homelessness in my country and in my church.

In December I had the opportunity to participate in a peace delegation to Israel and the Palestinian territories. There I experienced firsthand the suffering inflicted by war and injustice. I saw that suffering in the face of Claudette at Caritas in Jerusalem as she told her story symbolic of the fate of Palestinians in the whole region. "As a Palestinian, I am a refugee in my own city, expelled by the Israelis from my own home. When I was a child, my father rented the third floor of our house to an Israeli family. The Israeli daughter in the family and I became friends. Now my childhood friend lives in my house." I heard that suffering in the story of Tania, a twenty-four-year-old Russian Jew and a member of the Israeli Committee against House Demolitions. In Tania's simple, heartbreaking words, "House demolitions occur very early in the morning. Sometimes we stand in front of the bulldozers; sometimes we sit with the family." For her action Tania has been disowned by her Jewish family of origin. In so many of the stories there, we heard about the complicity of the United States in the injustice of the Israeli occupation. Returning from this experience, as our plane was making its final descent into the Newark airport, our captain announced, "I want to be the first to welcome you to the U.S." My eyes welled up; I knew that from now on, I would live in my U.S. home with the ache of homelessness.

We in LCWR leadership have the opportunity to participate in a variety of meetings where ecclesial issues are the content of our dialogue. During one meeting, our conversation turned to a discussion of the church's position on homosexuality. As some of the participants made their appeal to ethical directives based in natural law and the intrinsically disordered nature of homosexuality, I found myself tapping into a place of grief and alienation. In my heart's eye, I saw faces of men and women I know whose sexual orientation is gay or lesbian and who live compassionately, justly yearning for a return of compassion and justice on the part of a church they love. I thought of men and women whose passion for wholeness in relationship is lived in deep commitment to lifelong same-sex partners. I heard deep in my own being their struggle to find a home in our church. In the image of our two trees, I could feel my roots moving toward theirs and they leaning toward me as together we want nothing more than to shape a home space for those who are "other." Around that meeting table, I was compelled to speak on their behalf, to tell the story of the beauty of their relationships, and to offer an alternative ethic of sexuality. The moment felt frozen in time; I felt the ache of my own homelessness in the church that is my home.

And yet, as cruciform as it feels and is, the acute pain of homelessness is a gift. Where we do *not* fit, where we experience ourselves ostracized to the margins from our privileged place at the center, we are given the opportunity for transformation. Sallie McFague calls this a wild space, a space opened up by any rifts with the standard way of being, deciding, and acting. In her words, "It is the wild space in each of us, whatever does not fit the stereotypical human being, that questions the definition of the good life." The feeling of being an outsider in places we once called home is the wild space of our possibility.[6]

In the wild space we recognize the limitations of the self-sufficient power of the privileged and, like the older tree in our story, lean toward the more fragile, vulnerable, and less privileged. Our "power over" becomes "power with" in a compassion that creates a home for any and all who are other. Like Sophia-God, incarnated in Jesus, we set wildly inclusive tables in the household of God where our friends on the margins find a place of honor. Out of our home-lessness, we make a new home, where around tables with room for infinite expansion, we tell new stories of salvation.

I hear evidences of that wild space in some of our salvific actions:

♦ Last summer at this Assembly, we voiced our commitment to create and to participate in inclusive tables where laity, women and men religious, clerics, and bishops sit together to share our hopes for our church. In response to that desire the National Board designed a suggested process of "healing circles."

♦ In February, our executive committee endorsed a statement drafted by a collaborative group of individuals and organizations. The statement calls for a church that includes around its tables of conversation "silent subjects" as "active partners" and names these processes as being at the heart of healing in our church.

♦ At our May meeting of the Bishops' Committee for International Justice and Peace, an African doctor from Zambia told how the Zambian people, in collegial processes, decided not to accept genetically modified organisms even though such acceptance would have helped to alleviate the severity of their hunger.

I believe it was from my wild space of homelessness that I was able to say so clearly, "Doctor, your story challenges us to resolve the food distribution crisis in ways that give people the power to make the decisions that are true to them—culturally, politically, socially, ethically." I could feel the healing that fell between the doctor and me.

The thoughts of Elizabeth Johnson are appropriate here:

Women know the breakthrough of their own strength, usually under duress. The kind of power they evidence is a vitality, an empowering vigor that reaches out and awakens freedom and strength in oneself and others. It is an energy that brings forth, stirs up, and fosters life, enabling autonomy and friendship. It is a movement of spirit that builds, mends, struggles with and against, celebrates and laments. It transforms people and bonds them with one another and to the world. And it operates in a relational manner.

She describes those actions as "granting fragmentary experiences of salvation."[7]

If you listen, you'll hear—not just in the silent woods, but in the silence of this room—the secret of the trees, our secret: "Leaning can make you live forever and your weakest places can be someone else's home."

## Women Freed by an Embrace:
## Claiming the Liberating Power of Resurrection
## in the Embodiment of Truth-Telling

We turn now to our third story, the story of Karen Ridd and Marcela Rodriguez, arrested by the National Guard in El Salvador. Although we do not know what brought these two women to prison, we can surmise that it had something to do with the fierceness of their sense of relatedness to the people of El Salvador. More than a clue for that interpretation is found in the way they are with one another in an inseparable camaraderie. They cling to one another desiring that their freedom come together or not at all. Told boldly in their very bodies is the only truth that matters: against impossible odds, relatedness liberates. It is their unnerving authenticity that sets them free.

This story echoes with other stories of this year. I hear this story in Mercy Sister Moira Kenny, on trial for an act of civil disobedience at the SOA. "As a sister, my primary reason for taking part in the annual protest at the SOA is to honor the memory of Maura Clark, Ita Ford, Dorothy Kazel, and Jean Donovan. I also participate in order to stand in solidarity with my friend Jennifer Harbury whose Guatemalan husband was tortured for two years and killed by SOA grads. I took this action as an act of conscience."

I hear this story in the story of two women peace activists, Israeli Terry Greenblatt and Palestinian Amneh Badran, who are working together to bring women's perspectives to the Middle Eastern peace negotiations. In the words of Greenblatt, "We women assemble, sit on the same side of the table. We put the strife and pains in front of us, look at the male diplomats courageously, and come up with a win-win formula." They are both accused of being traitors, of being naïve and impractical daydreamers, but they persist in sitting side by side at the table as "long as it takes to achieve a peaceful solution."[8]

I hear this story in the story of three Dominicans, Carol Gilbert, Jackie Hudson, and Ardeth Platte, who, on October 6, 2002, the anniversary of the start of the war in Afghanistan, and with thousands of U.S. troops poised to overtake Baghdad, snipped through a chain-link fence on the site of the Minuteman silo near Greeley, Colorado. According to the article in the *Denver Post*, "Some say it was a charade. Some say it was a sacrilege. Some say it was idealism run amok." But for the sisters, the intent was clear: "We are people of conscience, required to bear witness."[9]

And I hear this story in us.

♦ A year ago at our Assembly we reiterated our call to "use our corporate voice and influence in solidarity with people who experience powerlessness or any other form of violence or oppression" (LCWR Goals). We reclaimed with greater clarity our desire to speak the truth of the Gospel more publicly in the media. We acknowledged that a more public witness on our part draws us as women religious into a place of deeper integrity, communion, and hope. As a presidency, Executive Committee, and National Board, we have honored that Conference desire by drafting statements and signing on to statements directed toward more just relationships within our church and our world. Sometimes, precisely because our approach is relational rather than adversarial, the media has chosen not to publish them. Our stories, too, insistent on relationships, resistant to the violence of dualisms, can be dismissed as irrelevant, naïve, hopelessly idealistic. Yet, we trust in the liberating power of holding on tenaciously to what is true for us.

◆ During our annual LCWR visitation to Rome in May, we deliberately chose, given the U.S. participation in the conflict, both in Iraq and the Middle East, to meet with the U.S. ambassador to the Vatican. It was out of our sense of relationship that we were able to name clearly the arrogance of the United States in the global arena and to speak our hope that our government will enter more humbly into relationships of sisterhood and brotherhood with the nations of the world. Our unequivocal description of U.S. policy as arrogant moved the ambassador to question that descriptive. His question opened up further conversation and engendered in us a sense that we had been heard.

◆ Also in Rome, our visits to the various offices were stories of truth telling in relationship. Although many of the meetings were challenging to the depth of my very soul, I celebrated with every fiber of my being our way of being present as women religious. We were women of integrity, calm, nondefensive, and well prepared. It was like being in a clear, blue pool of water. We spoke the truth of who we are and were firm in our communication that our expression of religious life is authentic, faithful to the direction of Vatican II and the inspiration of our founders. Something happened in those rooms in our clear and truthful speech freed to be so by the sure and certain relationships among us as LCWR leadership. I would never presume to call it transformation of the Roman Curia; I will, however, dare to name it respect.

For me, these stories are stories of resurrection. Very early in the morning, the women go together to the tomb. Whatever it is that they learn as they sit by that place of imprisonment together, they are afraid. I like to believe that, in the encouraging company of one another, they see clearly that they themselves are to be the ongoing presence of Jesus' inclusive way of life. They realize that, in so doing, they will bring upon themselves the costly judgment of the Roman government and the religious authorities. As did the soldiers in our core story of the women in the El Salvador prison, these resurrection women know that the powers that be do understand the power of "inseparable camaraderie." In their bodies become the body of the risen Christ they cling to one another, freed from religious and political entombment to proclaim the good news that the way of Jesus is alive in them.

These women live on in the resurrection story we tell by the truth of our lives.

## Celebrating the Power of our Sisterhood

Having let a nursing bear, leaning trees, and embracing women tell their stories and, in doing so, tell ours, I go back with gratitude to the ancient basswood tree that directed me, in the first place, to stay with these stories. As I sit on her trunk still firmly rooted in the earth and peer into the hollow, hallowed darkness of her crone-womb, I can feel her smile; she knows that I have discovered an irrevocable intimacy with her. This intimacy is born of the realization, made even more conscious through this reflection, that we women religious are living out of and growing more deeply into an ecofeminism that is a communion of companionship, responsibility, and accountability to the whole web of life. In the words of Ivone Gebara, "The first thing to be affirmed in an ecofeminist perspective is relatedness.

Relatedness is the primary reality: It is constitutive of all beings. It is the foundational reality of all that is or can exist."[10]

In this interrelated web of life, the whole system changes when there are even slight changes in patterns of relationship. Every act sourced in the power of genuine relatedness subverts the power of hierarchy and patriarchy. In the stories we have told this morning, we have uncovered within ourselves the power most necessary for the creation, salvation, and resurrection of our church, our world, and our earth. It is the power of relationship, of our sisterhood with all that is. This power is prophetic; it is the most radical act of dissent. With Clarissa Pinkola Estés,

> Let's admit it. We women are building a motherland; each with her own plot of soil eked from a night of dreams, a day of work. We are spreading this soil in larger and larger circles, slowly, slowly. One day it will be a continuous land, a resurrected land come back from the dead. This world is being made from our lives, our cries, our laughter, our bones. It is a world worth making, a world worth living in, a world in which there is a prevailing and decent wild sanity.[11]

*Members of the Executive Committee and regional chairs will come forward as their point of celebration is being read. Each will scoop up some soil from a container and spread the soil on the stage.*

- ◆ The Executive Committee celebrates the way we work together for the good of the Conference in a spirit of prayer, trust, honesty, attentiveness to one another, and genuine joy.

- ◆ Region 1 celebrates our Wisdom's Way project, whereby the linked resources of regional organizations and individual congregations provide support to women on welfare in their quest for an education.

- ◆ Region 2 celebrates the work of our Justice Committee, particularly our development of the Land Ethic and the corporate stance of our region against the war.

- Region 3 celebrates our establishment of the St. Katharine Drexel Mission Center and Shrine and the 100 percent affirmative vote creating the merger of the Ringwood Franciscans and the Sisters of St. Francis of Philadelphia.

- Region 4 celebrates our sponsorship of a tuition-free Catholic middle school for girls created by the collaboration of the Sisters of Mercy, the Sisters of Notre Dame de Namur, the School Sisters of Notre Dame, and the Bon Secours Sisters.

- Region 5 celebrates our sisterly presence in the northeastern Louisiana town of Lake Providence, where we provide salaries and housing for an interracial team of four sisters engaged in a wide variety of ministries.

- Region 6 celebrates our Founders Project, the collaboration of eight congregations in the Cincinnati area, in providing a van that transports persons in neglected neighborhoods to doctors' offices, clinics, and hospitals.

- Region 7 celebrates our witness to the power of collaboration as our leadership teams and our congregational justice coordinators share resources in responding to the war in Iraq, gathering others to pray with us for peace, and taking public action.

- Region 8 celebrates our Billboard Project, a collaborative effort of leadership and Communications Directors resulting in Chicago area billboards proclaiming, "Peace Because Good Planets Are Hard to Find," and signed the "Catholic Sisters in your area."

- Region 9 celebrates our sisters imprisoned for their actions of conscience at the SOA: Sister Kathleen Long, Sinsinawa Dominican; Sister Caryl Hartjes, Sister of St. Agnes; and Sister Dorothy Pagosa, Stevens Point Franciscan.

- Region 10 celebrates our Intercommunity Environmental Council, a group of fifteen St. Louis–area religious congregations working together to raise awareness around ecological issues.

- Region 11 celebrates in a poem:

  > Women religious crisscrossing the horizon,
  > Partnerships creating access:
  > To the needs of life,
  > The seeds of life planted in holy ground.
  > Education, health care, the arts.
  > All is holy: the people native to the land;
  > The newcomer shaking your hand;
  > The poor, the wealthy;
  > The sick, the healthy.
  > Those giving birth;
  > Those flowering the earth;
  > All is holy, especially the folks who live there!

- Region 12 celebrates our Border Projects, including meeting annually on the border with Mexico in solidarity with *maquiladora* workers and women religious ministering in the area and supporting an intercongregational Border Projects Fund for systemic change.

- Region 13 celebrates our ongoing commitment to encourage right relationships with our bishops by sitting at table with them and emphasizing the importance of the role of women in our dioceses and in the larger church.

- Region 14 celebrates our involvement in the plight of incarcerated women, particularly the awning we made possible for inmates at the California Institution for Women in Corona. The awning covers the area where women receive their daily meals.

- Region 15 celebrates our Intercommunity Ministry Volunteer Program providing volunteers of all ages opportunities to live and minister with Catholic religious communities in service with the poor.

They were nothing more than people, by themselves. Even paired, any pairing, they would have been nothing more than people by themselves. But all together, they have become the heart and muscles of something perilous and new, something strange and growing and great. Together, all together, they are the instruments of change.[12]

## Notes

1. Barbara Kingsolver, *Small Wonder* (New York: HarperCollins, 2002).

2. Megan McKenna and Tony Cowan, *Keepers of the Story* (Maryknoll, NY: Orbis Books, 1997).

3. Reprinted with permission in *Leading from Within*, LCWR 2001, originally printed in *The Other Side* (May–June 1990).

4. Clarissa Pinkola Estés, "You Were Made for This"; see http://www.wanttoknow.info/youweremadeforthis.

5. Dorothee Soelle, *The Silent Cry: Mysticism and Resistance* (Minneapolis: Fortress Press, 2001).

6. Sally McFague, *Life Abundant, Rethinking Theology and Economy for a Planet in Peril* (Minneapolis: Fortress, 2001), 48.

7. Elizabeth Johnson, *She Who Is* (New York: Crossroad, 1992).

8. Anat Cohen, Wenews correspondent, Jerusalem.

9. Diane Carman, *Denver Post*, April 6, 2003.

10. Ivonne Gebara, *Longing for Running Water: Ecofeminism and Liberation* (Minneapolis: Fortress, 1999).

11. Clarissa Pinkola Estés, quoted in Alice Walker, *Absolute Trust in the Goodness of the Earth: New Poems* (New York: Random House, 2003).

12. Keri Hulme, *The Bone People* (New York: Penguin, 1983).

# 8

## 2008 National Assembly
### "On This Holy Mountain"

# MIDWIFING
# A VIBRANT FUTURE

## *Mary Whited, CPPS*

— Denver, August 4, 2008 —

*By the time Mary Whited called upon the image of a mountain to begin
her presidential address, Earth had taken center stage in world events that
riveted the attention of even the most skeptical observer.*

*A powerful tsunami in Southeast Asia and a devastating hurricane
named Katrina swept away lives, shorelines, and neighborhoods. Believers and deniers debated the reality of climate change while food and water
shortages escalated worldwide. Oil prices swung high and low; opinion
remained divided on the development of offshore oil drilling and shale oil
development. Abusers of detainees in Baghdad's Abu Ghraib prison were
court martialed and convicted. The fugitive president of Iraq was captured and sentenced to death. U.S. headlines featured news of a fence
being built along the Mexican border, financial bailouts of ailing corporations, a stock market plunge, and the election of Barack Obama as the
first African American president. A Supreme Court decision recharged the
national debate on gun control.*

*The new pope, Benedict XVI, visited the United States and spoke
with victims of clergy sexual abuse; five dioceses declared bankruptcy.
Arguments flared over whether politicians could be denied Communion
on the basis of their stance on abortion. As the LCWR prepared to mark
its fiftieth anniversary with the "Women & Spirit" exhibition, the Stonehill*

*Symposium in Massachusetts on apostolic religious life since Vatican II sounded an alarm concerning the direction of religious life in general and of the LCWR in particular.*

*The Exodus story of the Egyptian midwives, with which Mary Whited began her presidential address, encourages "a communal, reconciling, contemplative, and hopeful perspective" amid times that challenged LCWR members to "tend the places where new life is stirring."*

—◆—

We come to the mountains to gain perspective. At this height the view is spectacular, the air is fresh, and the beauty takes one's breath away. Being at a mile-high altitude has a way of expanding our vision, deepening our sensitivities, and surfacing our priorities. Our sacred story is replete with others who had the courage and the stamina to climb: the Chosen People who sealed a covenant with Yahweh, a prophet who spoke boldly on behalf of the oppressed, and a Samaritan woman who conversed with a Messiah about where her ancestors worshiped. On a mountain, Jesus was transfigured in the presence of his disciples, and followers of Jesus learned the way of the Beatitudes. Jesus went up to Jerusalem to die and to rise.

In that tradition, we, women religious leaders, gather on this holy mountain to step back and to take a long look at these key questions that churn deep down in our hearts: How do we attend to this moment in the life of our congregations and our leadership conference? How do we "midwife" religious life into a future that is unfolding even as we assemble? How do we encourage our members to hold on to what is needed and to let go of what is not essential so that we are freer to climb? Can we risk conversing about the hopes and fears that stir in our hearts? Are there other mountains we need to be climbing? Are the mountains we are scaling even worth the climb?

I began to reflect on this address by calling upon some wonderful women whose life-giving perspectives helped to reframe difficult realities into situations of hope. There were so many—Catherine of Siena, Philippine Duchesne, Elizabeth Ann Seton, Theresa Weber, the Hebrew midwives Puah and Shiphrah, whose courage, imagination, and daring are highlighted in the very first chapter of Exodus. Let's listen to their story:

> The king of Egypt spoke to Shiphrah and Puah, the two mid-wives who assisted the Hebrew women. "When you help the Hebrew women give birth," he said to them, "kill the baby if it is a boy; but if it is a girl, let her live." But the midwives were God-fearing and so did not obey the king; instead, they let the boys live. So the king sent for the midwives and asked them, "Why are you doing this? Why are you letting the boys live?" They answered, "The Hebrew women are not like Egyptian women; they give birth easily, and their babies are born before either of us gets there." Because the midwives were God-fearing, God was good to them and made them fruitful. [Another translation says, "God made them heroes." (Exod. 1:15–21)

These midwives are incredible! They speak to power on behalf of God's people who are unable to speak for themselves. Finding a different way to respond to the orders of Pharaoh and conversing directly with him guarantee new life and fresh hope for the people of God. Being the responsible leaders they are, these midwives seek to ensure both a safe delivery of Hebrew children and a vital future for the people of God. The history of salvation lies in their hands. Shiphrah and Puah cannot be silent with a shared future at stake. New life must be birthed, whatever that takes!

How often it is the sacred work of women to present an alternative to the dominant culture that exerts control over others! Puah and Shiphrah are up to the task as they embrace the vulnerable, suffering, frustrated, hurting, and weary people of Yahweh. Alignment with Yahweh is essential to nurturing dreams. The midwives' alignment with Yahweh is key to delivering new life and birthing new hope among the people chosen by Yahweh. The midwives realize that Pharaoh's command will lead to the demise of God's people, yet their attention is not on diminishment. They focus on delivering new life and nurturing hope! Some would call this stance prophetic. Rabbi Abraham Heschel describes a prophet as one who "combines a very deep love, a very powerful dissent, and a powerful resolve with envisioning hope." Shiphrah and Puah's love for God's people, their courageous dissent, and the resolve to nurture new life, whatever it takes, all clear the path toward a vision of hope among the people of Yahweh. This stance is prophetic!

Sitting with these wonderful leaders and companions on the journey, I marvel at how Shiphrah and Puah can reframe a seemingly hopeless situation into a life-giving reality. Their wisdom and their deep caring about the future of God's people allow them to face this frightening question that must have lurked in their hearts: What will it take for this remnant to flourish? If Puah and Shiphrah were here today, I wonder what they might say to us to whom leadership has been entrusted. What new perspectives could they offer us in our attempts to lead our people? How would they support new life and stir hope in our congregations, our church, the world, and, especially, in the places of ache and weariness within our own spirits? Surely they would encourage us. Surely they would remind us, "Tend the places where new life is stirring." Perhaps they would challenge us to lead from a midwife's perspective—a communal, reconciling, contemplative, and hopeful perspective.

## Communal Perspective

For women religious, nurturing new life is a communal enterprise. Side by side. Shoulder to shoulder. Face to face. Like Puah and Shiphrah. Assisting in the birth of new life requires sharing dreams and imagining together. As the Leadership Conference of Women Religious, we know these patterns so well. When we began to engage in the process of our "Shared Future," we reflected on these powerful words:

> What we do together as leaders: sharing our personal visions, clarifying what is important to us, learning to see with new eyes, unearthing our mental models, creating the capacity

to think together, and making new connections is an act of hope and imagination that has a life beyond ourselves and our time.[1]

As a leadership conference, we imagined together how best to address the devastation from Hurricane Katrina. And new life is blossoming in New Orleans! On our fiftieth anniversary, our leadership conference initiated a traveling exhibit to celebrate the dreams of Catholic sisters from the time they stepped foot in our country. *Women & Spirit: Catholic Sisters in America* is coming to birth in artifacts, sound, color, and printed words. To not remember the determination and faith of women religious working together would surely neglect their tremendous contribution to church and society. To not tell the stories of those who have paved the way before us would surely create a vacuum in our legacy and fail to highlight a powerful story of delivering new life.

When congregations imagine the future together, our work is labor intensive. Because birthing a new reality is a difficult, focused process, it should not be rushed. Rightly so, the mergers, reconfigurations, and development or divestment of properties require a tremendous amount of discernment as well as leaders' attentiveness. And shifts in ways of organizing create new opportunities for a community, or for our leadership conference, to dream together. Organizational changes are significant and do require our time and energy; however, we miss the point if these changes fail to deepen our commitment to one another and our determination to stay with the climb. They miss the point if they fail to rekindle the passion so needed to birth new life now and into the future.

In the past several months I have had a recurring dream. Details change, but the patterns remain the same. I am wending my way from room to room in old, familiar surroundings like our motherhouse, which dates back to 1875, or my grandparents' home. I suddenly find myself in a maze of rooms I have never stepped foot into before. The surroundings are unfamiliar. I feel alone and hesitate to take another step. I'm tempted to retreat, and I glance back over my shoulder. The rooms from which I have come have vanished. I can no longer go back. I am aware of a Mysterious Presence who urges me forward. I relax and take the next step. And another. And another. I sense that I am being led.

Many times I have tried to unravel the many layers of meaning in these dreams. For me, of course, but perhaps for us as well. Leadership sometimes feels like walking through a maze, working our way through the complexities and challenges that confront us each and every day. Along the way we encounter strong forces, within ourselves or among our members, to stay with what we know. Yet, strength to move forward comes from a sense of being grounded and knowing we are not alone. We must go forward together, even when "forward together" might seem like a circling back. Didn't the Hebrew people wander in the desert for forty years before reaching the Promised Land? Can you, too, sense the Mysterious Presence who invites us to take another step? Do you, too, sense that we are being led?

Puah and Shiphrah did not realize their conversation with Pharaoh would lead to the exodus out of Egypt into the wilderness. Their risking prods us on. And as we walk, we leave behind our familiar motherhouses, provinces, structures that have served us well, and ways of living and ministering that deter us from being together. We grieve deeply when older members die. We ask "why?" when death plucks younger, vibrant members of our communities from active ministry and vital community living. Amid the "lettings go," we risk the exodus journey. Drawn forward by the Mysterious Presence, we are led into the desert, the place of ultimate trust.

In the desert we are invited to address the very essence of our lives as women religious and to reclaim our identity as God's Chosen People. Together we honestly seek to name what is happening within and among us and how we feel about this climb. We talk about the cost of leaving Egypt, and we grieve what we have left behind. We open our dreams to one another, and we share the fears of today and our hopes for tomorrow. We attend to the deep yearning to belong that never goes away. In the desert we look for life in places that seem barren. Possibly we discover there are some things we should have left in Egypt. Possibly we reclaim what we have lost along the way. And perhaps we come to see that being together on the journey touches the core identity of who we are today and who we will be tomorrow—women of God, ecclesial women, a community chosen by God, and midwives of a future that unfolds in us even as we climb together.

## Reconciling Perspective

The charism of my community, the Sisters of the Most Precious Blood, is to be Christ's reconciling presence. Reconciliation colors how I see myself within the church. And so I often wonder: What will it take to heal a painfully divided church? I hold the weariness of women who can't find their voices in a church they love and serve. I hold the frustrations of persons and groups who are disregarded, labeled, or divided into camps because of differing perspectives: liberal/conservative, right/left, people of God/institutional church, religious who live an "authentic" religious life/those who don't. Anyone who has climbed a mountain knows that the top can be reached by various paths. So what will it take to embrace the differences? What will it take to span the gaps?

Puah and Shiphrah recognize that new life can be born only by conversing with Pharaoh. They weigh their possibilities of talking with Pharaoh against the greater risks of keeping silent, confronting, opting out, or acquiescing to Pharaoh's wishes. They know that countering power with the same kind of power might restrain it, but, in the end, that will not lead to peace.[2] Speaking to a dominating power in kind will only jeopardize any hope of delivering new life. Not as victims, but out of integrity and from a different perspective, they speak with Pharaoh. They have no hope of changing Pharaoh's mind or transforming his oppressive regime. Yet their actions, and their refusal to act on Pharaoh's order, pave the way for new life to be born and hope to stir among God's Chosen People.

What will it take to bring a reconciling perspective to a painfully divided church? This past year our presidency has continued to engage in significant conversations with Vatican officials, U.S. bishops, and the Council of Major Superiors of Women Religious. We bring our perspectives as women religious, and the LCWR, to each of these groups. In talking with the Vatican, hope lies in our willingness and determination to stay in the conversation for the long haul and to not lose heart. As we talk with U.S. bishops, hope lies in our addressing together issues of concern: causes of migration and rights for immigrants, an end to wars in Afghanistan and Iraq, relief for those who have suffered natural disasters, and the primacy of life. As we talk with the Council of Major Superiors of Women Religious and experience different understandings of church and different expressions of religious life, hope lies in a willingness to explore the common ground on which we stand as women who are religious.

Such efforts do not ignore past or present hurts. We remember, but we remember differently. We stay in the conversation so that women religious do not become merely an adjunct to the church. We are ecclesial women who love a church that is both institution and the people of God. If we do not claim both, we lose a prophetic edge as well as any hope of healing the rifts. Spanning the gaps is a matter of the heart even more than a matter of the head. Closing the gaps requires a "heartfelt" response toward reconciliation and healing.

Walter Brueggemann writes: "It is the vocation of the prophet to keep alive the ministry of imagination, to keep on conjuring and proposing future alternatives to the single one the king wants to urge as the only thinkable one."[3] Puah and Shiphrah imagine an alternative to what Pharaoh orders. Wise midwives that they are, they know when to push and when to simply breathe. Their reconciling perspective urges us to engage in the difficult and honest conversations, to imagine alternatives that can bridge the gaps, to acknowledge our part in perpetuating the divisions, to cultivate unity even as we speak the truth, and, perhaps most importantly, to know when to push and when to simply breathe.

## Contemplative Perspective

Let us take a moment to sit in silence and breathe deeply together. [*Pause.*] For the realities we hold require not only a depth but also a breadth that cannot be reached by sitting alone. As leaders sit together in silence, wisdom emerges, compassion grows and we support each other in labor. Together we hold our concerns about the present and our anxieties about the future of religious life, the church, the world, and the earth. Beyond a sense of duty, we touch into the call and the privilege of being leaders today. We prioritize our deepest beliefs and focus energy in the places that have most potential for new life. We sense our alignment with that Mysterious Presence who accompanies us up this mountain. We gain the confidence that God's Chosen will be sustained in exile. In contemplation, we meet the Puahs and the Shiphrahs within who long to deliver new life. We hear the voices of these midwives address the pharaoh that lies within—who needs to control, who attempts to dominate, or who resists being transformed by the circumstances of our lives and by the grace of God. We find our voices and the willingness to speak our truth with love. Alignment with the Sacred deepens the integrity out of which we speak to the pharaohs in our church and world.

As leaders, this is our time, and we are the ones called to lead the climb. The daily pressures and complexities with which we deal often slow the climb. We seek times and spaces in our busy lives to pause and breathe with other climbers who yearn for peace of mind and heart. We sit together, attending to who we are becoming in the midst of all we do. In contemplation, we hold the weariness and suffering in both church and world. We tend to the new life that stirs—within, among, and around us.

Contemplation takes us inward. It also takes us to the mountains where we behold the earth as a sacred place and see how humanity is embedded in the earth. From this perspective we find ourselves connected to both the hopes and anguish of the people of our world and the groaning of creation. On this holy mountain we are the consciousness of the globe and at times, even of the universe. At this height, the gaps seem less significant, and the possibilities of closing the gaps increase. We cease praying to the God who will keep us safe. Instead, we dwell with a Mystery who invites us to risk. Serenity is no longer enough. We are called to responsible action. Dorothee Soelle describes the shift in perspective: "What really happens in mystical union is not a new vision of God but a different relationship to the world—one that has borrowed the eyes of God."[4] This perspective creates the capacity for hope!

## Hopeful Perspective

When pain becomes overwhelming, it is easy for numbness to settle in. Yet Puah and Shiphrah are not numb to the despair of God's people. They enter the pain and anguish so that they can advocate on behalf of those who suffer. When they speak to Pharaoh, they express neither anger nor rage but speak with a "candor born of anguish and passion."[5] Brueggemann claims that the primary calling of a prophet is not to be an angry social critic. Instead a prophet is someone who is willing to take an honest look at upsetting and unsettling realities that are ignored by society at large and the powers that be.[6] The midwives pierce a numbness that keeps God's people powerless!

Today it is so easy to become numb to the growing poverty across the globe. (How can anyone grasp the immensity of it all, much less do something about it?) It is so easy to become numb to the increasing numbers of Iraqi refugees; to the migration of peoples who are searching to meet their basic, human needs; to the women and children who are trafficked and terrorized each and every day. (There is too much to do. How much farther can we be stretched? Our resources are limited.) It is so easy to become numb to the global realities of climate change and ecological devastation. (We try to recycle. Isn't that enough?) It is so easy to become numb to the violence on our local streets. (It's brought into our living rooms between commercials.) Who will pierce the numbness? We, women religious, are aware and have access to the suffering of people all over the globe. Are we up to the challenge of piercing the numbness? Are we up to the challenge of delivering new life on behalf of those who feel hopeless? We, who realize that all is connected, know that, when we hold the suffering and weariness of those whose lives we touch each and every day, we pierce the numbness in our society, our church, our world and, especially, within our own congregations of women religious.

But we cannot pierce the numbness alone. The complexity of the global challenges we face requires combining our efforts with partners and collaborators. Donna Markham said, "We need each other to test out ideas, to share what we're learning, to help us see in new ways, to listen to our stories. We need each other to forgive us when we fail, to trust us with their dreams, to offer their hope when we've lost our own."[7] According to Meg Wheatley, "the world doesn't change one person at a time. It changes as networks of relationships form among people who discover they share a common cause and vision of what's possible."[8] As a leadership conference, linking our efforts with other groups and conferences, such as the Conference of Major Superiors of Men, the Canadian Religious Conference, and the Conference of Latin American Religious enables us, collectively and consciously, to address global challenges in very strategic ways. Together we discover leverage points for change!

Realizing our deeper connections to those who are hungry moves us to say no to hunger. Recognizing our deeper connections not only to those who are being terrorized but also to those who are terrorizing stirs us to say no to the terrorism. When we connect our energies around a resolution directed toward climate change, we say no to environmental devastation. In the process, we come to see how we are integrally connected to one another and to the earth. As we speak to and act on any issue, we discover how that issue is intertwined with so many other issues. In opening our eyes and hearts to the sufferings of our world, hope can be awakened, a hope that allows us to see from the perspective of God. Midwives never settle for a future that is less than hopeful. This is the price for being aware. Midwives never settle down. This is the price for growth in compassion. Midwives never settle in. This is the price for being channels of hope.

Channels of hope! We stay at the climb in the footsteps of those women religious who have scaled the mountain before us. Since the skills of midwifery must be passed down from one generation to the next, we feel a responsibility to those women religious who will come after us and who we invite to join in the climb. They too will voice their truth, probably different from our own, and pay the price so that God's visions and dreams can surely be born anew.

Beyond the first few verses of Exodus, we hear no more of Puah and Shiphrah. These midwives deliver new life and then, like us, let others take the lead. But they leave behind a communal, reconciling, contemplative, and hopeful perspective to assist the next leaders who will also climb the mountain. In the end, the value of climbing a mountain is not measured by the numbers who climb, but rather by a remnant of Chosen People who stay the climb with hope, determination, and passion. After all, hope "is never generated among us but always given to us. And whenever it is given we are amazed."[9]

These days we, women religious leaders, gather together "On This Holy Mountain." As we meet, perhaps we are gaining some perspective on how God is leading us personally and together as this Leadership Conference of Women Religious. We become aware that, in each of us and among all of us, there lives a midwife who is both mystic and prophet.[10] She aligns with God toward comforting the weary, attending to dreams, speaking to power, reconciling gaps, piercing the numbness, and nurturing new life, whatever the costs. She supports our resolve to continue the climb—shoulder to shoulder, face to face, side by side, step by step, like Shiphrah and Puah. She tends to labor and birth. She keeps us climbing when we are weary, and she helps us let go of what hinders the climb. She is present to us as we gather here. She is fanning the slightest stirrings of hope!

Climbing the mountain has become a way of life for ecclesial women who desire to see from the perspective of God. These days we open ourselves to a new moment of grace when that Mysterious

Presence, whom we call Spirit of God, leads and supports us in climbing the mountain. In her presence, we will not be deterred from the heart work and head work that are essential to climbing.

As the Leadership Conference of Women Religious, we hold a "Shared Future," a future that is not only beyond us but also resides within and among us. We shape this future as we sit together and share our dreams and visions of what is possible. The Spirit is with us. She will help us give voice to what lies in our hearts. She will rekindle the flame when the fire goes down. We cannot be silent with so much at stake—the future unfolding for women religious. Hope seeking rebirth "On This Holy Mountain"!

## Notes

1. Introduction to Process of LCWR Shared Future, 2008.

2. Robert Schreiter, *The Ministry of Reconciliation: Spirituality and Strategies* (Maryknoll, NY: Orbis Books, 1998), 29.

3. Walter Brueggemann, *The Prophetic Imagination* (Minneapolis: Fortress, 2001), 40.

4. Dorothee Soelle, *The Silent Cry: Mysticism and Resistance* (Minneapolis: Fortress, 2001), 273.

5. Brueggemann, *The Prophetic Imagination*, 45.

6. Ibid., 3.

7. Donna Markham, "The Leader's Mantle: Creating Connection in Chaotic Times," Toronto, Ontario: University of St. Michael's College, Kelly Lecture, November 18, 2004.

8. Margaret Wheatley and Deborah Frieze, "Using Emergence to Take Social Innovation to Scale," 2006. http://www.margaretwheatley.com.

9. Brueggemann, *The Prophetic Imagination*, 79.

10. Mary Ruth Broz and Barbara Flynn, *Midwives of an Unnamed Future: Spirituality for Women in Times of Unprecedented Change* (Skokie, IL: Acta Publications, 2006), 174.

## Bibliography

Gittins, Anthony. *A Presence That Disturbs: A Call to Radical Discipleship.* Liguori, MO: Liguori/Triumph, 2002.

Prevallet, Elaine. *Making the Shift: Seeing Faith through a New Lens.* Nerinx, KY, 2006.

Senge, Peter, C., Otto Scharmer, Joseph Jaworski, and Betty Sue Flowers. *Presence: An Exploration of Profound Change in People, Organizations, and Society.* New York: Doubleday, 2004.

Sylvester, Nancy, and Mary Jo Klick, eds. *Crucible for Change: Engaging Impasse through Communal Contemplation and Dialogue.* Boerne, TX: Sor Juana, 2004.

Zaragoza, Rufino. *Longing Heart.* Portland, OR: OCP, 2002.

# 9

## 2010 National Assembly
### "Hope in the Midst of Darkness"
#### (Exploring the Ecclesial Role of Women Religious)

# CALLED TO HOPE AS PROPHETS, ARTISTS, HEALERS, AND LOVERS

## Marlene Weisenbeck, FSPA

— Dallas, August 13, 2010 —

*In her introductory remarks, Marlene Weisenbeck summarized the milieu in which LCWR members gathered for their 2010 Assembly and articulated a framework for response: prophecy, art, healing, and love.*

*These "holy energies" offered hope amid the events unfolding worldwide and in the United States, including debates on global warming and torture during interrogation. Banking and debt crises spread across Europe; Israeli forces attacked a relief flotilla attempting to reach Gaza. Californians affirmed Proposition 8 restricting marriage recognition to opposite-sex couples. These were the years of "Don't Ask, Don't Tell," identity theft, Wikileaks, and the birth of the Tea Party. There were glimmers of hope for women subject to honor killings in India and genital mutilation in Africa. For the first time in the United States a woman served as Speaker of the House. The last U.S. combat troops left Iraq, Al Qaeda presence increased in Yemen, and Muslims experienced growing hostility when they planned to build a mosque near Ground Zero in Lower Manhattan.*

*The Vatican announcement of an apostolic visitation to "look into the quality of the life" of women's religious institutes in the United States was swiftly followed by another declaring the launch of a "doctrinal assessment" of the "activities and initiatives" of the LCWR. Tensions rose as the Catholic*

*Health Association (CHA) supported the passage of the Affordable Care Act, while the U.S. bishops' conference opposed its passage. LCWR presidents met with the executive committee of the Council of Major Superiors of Women Religious in continuing efforts at reconciliation.*

*Calling upon wide-ranging models of energy, wisdom, and inspiration—including Mary Daniel Turner, SNDdeN; and Sandra Schneiders, IHM; Walter Brueggemann; and Leonard Bernstein—this address challenges its audience to "shore up the foundations that make hope possible."*

—✺—

Good morning, my friends, my sisters, and leaders for religious life, our church, our country, our world!

In 2009 we left New Orleans having celebrated our contribution to renewed life after Katrina and with J. Lora Dambroski, OSF, bidding us:

♦ to recover a deepened understanding of our LCWR Call by living out of an honest spirituality and theology of religious life rooted in the Gospel of Jesus—the hallmark of the LCWR Call that had just been reaffirmed along with the Shared Futures conversations that give it shape;

♦ to engender fresh creativity in the chaos of our time while not debasing our own expressions of faithfulness;

♦ to be carriers of the hope and an expression of Jesus' love and passion for life; and

♦ to pray to know the direction of the Spirit.[1]

Since then, we have experienced a year of contrasts and unexpected events. We have taken pride in the ongoing "Women & Spirit" exhibits, supported the efforts of the CHA for health care reform, hailed the courage of Bishop Kevin Dowling in South Africa, and enjoyed honored recognition from the U.S. House of Representatives, the Chicago mayor and city council, and Pax Christi. We also found ourselves quavering with the continuing ecclesial inquiries and canonical assessments, shocked by the planetary quakes in Haiti and Chile, Turkey and Mexico, the Gulf oil spill, floods in Pakistan, and disturbed by emerging news about sex abuse scandals around the world—not to mention the quakes that health care reform generated within our church and country. Few of these latter events were explosions of holy joy as happened at the resurrection!

Amid all the systemic unrest that these explosive events engender, we have called ourselves to "Hope in the Midst of Darkness." We dare to articulate how our ecclesial role as women religious is calling us to mission. We do not have to mimic our founders to find the answer about how to do this. St. Francis said, "I have done what is mine to do. May Christ show you what is yours." In other words, the Gospel will show us what to do, how we must act with the attitude of Jesus who emphasized an inclusive love of all in right relationships.

So, we ask ourselves over and over, "What is hope?" A high-tech sales consultant, Rick Page, says: "Hope is not a strategy and somewhere is not a destination." Business requires a plan and a strategy with concrete objectives. We should not think, in other words, that hope will get us where we want to be. Others will say that the essence of hope is changeless because the future is always new! The future itself is a revelation of God's desire for us. Like a certain nameless pastor who declared that authority in the church "doesn't rely on a formal imposition of hands, but rather a divine imperative from the heart," we can say also that hope is an imperative of the heart.[2]

Peter's first letter to early Christian communities echoes into our time: "In your hearts honor Christ the Lord as holy, always being prepared to make a defense to anyone who asks you for a reason for the hope that is in you; yet do it with gentleness and respect, having a good conscience, so that, when you are slandered, those who revile your good behavior in Christ may be put to shame" (1 Pet. 3:15–16).

## Called to Hope

Though we know instinctively the hope within us, we must give a reason for it. "Giving an account" means moving from a tentative, unspoken, fuzzy, or intuitive grasp of what fits for us as women religious, to a disciplined, articulate, and explicit description of that outlook so that others can understand and appropriate it for themselves. We must get the word out that Jesus Christ is the center of our lives, that generosity and goodness are what the world thirsts for, that difference, diversity, and dialogue are not dirty words but central to Trinitarian life at the heart of human relationships in community.[3] We must be a testimony of hope for the world. *Gaudium et Spes* states, in a clarion way, the future of humanity is in the hands of those who are capable of providing others a hopeful vision of life (*Gaudium et Spes*, 1).

The challenge is awesome. We reach for a way of living that expresses God's desires for us and all of creation. This requires of us to let God be as big as God wants to be—fluid, flexible, and ever-creating—and courageous abandonment to divine recklessness! Though reason and dialectic point the way for us, spiritual realities do not come largely through reasoning. They are reached through direct contact and participation in eternal realities. Ancient texts by Plato and about Socrates speak about those who mediate the spiritual world. They are prophets, artists, healers, and lovers. I would like to propose that hope calls us to respond to our time through a fourfold mission of prophecy, art, healing, and love.[4]

## Prophecy

John Paul II in *Vita Consecrata* stated:

> The prophetic character of consecrated life . . . takes the shape of *a special form of sharing in Christ's prophetic office, which the Holy Spirit communicates to the whole People of God. There is a prophetic dimension which belongs to the consecrated life as such, resulting from the radical nature of the following of Christ and of the subsequent dedication to the mission characteristic of the consecrated life.* (*Vita Consecrata* 84, emphasis added)

We are impelled by the Spirit who in mystical exhortation moves us forward in a prophetic way. Our primal place of relationship with our Creator is where we enter into the evolutionary process of creating our own Word as it is formed in us through Christ. Mysticism and prophecy are integral to one another in a dynamic process where the Spirit confirms our reading of reality and where the hands of our heart touch the ones needing compassion. It is necessary to discover the "art" of touching the heart and holding the hands of the victims of injustice while also calling to truth the authors of scandal. Hiding behind bushes will not do it. To go out from hiding is to have the courage to walk forth with a vitality that will protect the fecundity of our charisms. This will not be done without a living intimacy with Christ, and without ambiguity.

Prophecy gives us the capacity to be watching the horizons. Hope finds expression in prophetic daring where our charisms are exchanged within a present reality so that we can sow the seeds of justice with compassion. Central to the process is trust and solidarity, openness to assist one another, and rootedness in our mystical connectedness with God, who keeps us together and on the move.[5]

We might say that prophecy is about hearing the music of the future. Faith is dancing to it. Without some vision of the future as sacred, what would be the reason for compassion, sacrifice, and mutual care? The prophetic call is an individual quest for the holy that must lead to a communal quest for justice. As prophets for the future who move beyond pessimism and a culture of guilt and blame, we are prompted to see possibilities for healing, forgiveness, and to reenact the actions of Christ as he witnessed to God's tenderness. We bring our grain of sand in the wisdom of small steps that give imagination to charity.

*Vita Consecrata* states that true prophecy is born of mystical listening to God in the dialogue of prayer and proclaiming with our lives and lips the Gospel of Christ (VC 84). As our Jewish brothers and sisters regard the Torah as having seventy faces, which allows an interpretation of the Word in seventy ways, we too should never settle on one interpretation of the Gospel. Every generation must hear the Word of God for its own time.[6] Our lives as ecclesial women should be provocative. We must not despair of the impasse of nonexistent and misunderstood conversations with church leaders. Our mystical and prophetic traditions compel us to look into the darkness and to see what it reveals in terms of wisdom and insight. We are constantly led to attentiveness to what is on the brink (not to sleep), to grasping the moment we have, to trusting with others while not knowing the end, and to accepting risk together (never alone). Prophecy comes out of shared pain and emergency, not because we need to wallow in it but because we are in solidarity for the beginning of an alternative future. God will come into this tent with us because God knows we are good. Walter Brueggemann asserts that our voices will sound God's Word efficaciously after all the so-called "final voices of legitimacy have either been exposed as false or accommodated in silence."[7]

As leaders, how will we provide a way forward to the calls we are hearing in a time of uncertainty so that all can move to a fuller prophetic justice that God desires for the world?

## Art

Passion is a mysterious struggle at the center of all creativity. Henry James described it this way: "We work in the dark—we do what we can—we give what we have. Our doubt is our passion, and our passion is our task. The rest is the madness of art."[8] As artists, we must learn not to control this journey of mystery.

Because the artist is in dialogue with the Source of all creativity, art is the fruit of divine inspiration. Rising like the beauty of the dawn, our holy imaginations and expressions of song, dance, and poetry help us become an actor in the scene of divine goodness. It is about connecting the prose and the passion of the human journey which help people identify a spirituality (personalism, identity, contemplation, reflection) to assist them in navigating the challenges of modernity (e.g., technology and anonymity). An artist is not consumed by the past but by the empty space ahead of her. When Stanley Drucker, the renowned clarinetist in the New York Philharmonic, was about to retire, someone asked him, "What are you going to do?" He answered, "What I've always done; I'm going to play. I'm a player." And we too can say, "We are players in the divine symphony of love."

In scene 1 of Olivier Messiaen's opera *Saint François d'Assise*, Francis explains to Brother Leo that for the love of Christ he must patiently endure all contradictions, all suffering, and that this is "Perfect Joy."[9] St. Francis's lyrical affectivity cannot be dismissed. He abandoned himself to joy, not to misery. His instinct was for a prayer of praise over petition. As a humble *poverello*, he wrote new songs, rejoiced, exulted, and even danced before the pope. If we are to follow in this way, we will discover that our mission must be expressed in poetry, the poetry of hospitality, of savoring diversity, and in the ultimate aesthetics of charity, meekness, joy, and justice.

Tony Gittens, CSSp, reminds us that we are meant to sing with one another. We sing with our lungs and limbs filled and gifted with God's bounteous grace. Paraphrasing Thomas Hardy, he notes that we are like the thrush; we may be "darkling" people. But we can fill our lungs and fling our souls on a world in need, irrespective of the "growing gloom," because we, like the bird "in blast-beruffled plume," are called and destined to do so, and like the thrush, we are inspired by "some blessed Hope."[10]

In our baptism we are called to be light. If we allow ourselves to be led literally and symbolically to the altar of God, then we too assent to being wrapped in colorful cloths and thrown into the myriad design of stained glass prisms. We are invited to dance upon common ground, the reflection of the living God we experience in one another. Hand grasping hand, we are radiant for we are all hues of hope![11] Hope in emerging beauty enables the artist to face an empty canvas, a musician to put notes on a five-lined sheet, and ultimately, as Pope Benedict says, "to become a custodian of beauty in the world. Dramatic beauty becomes a proclamation of hope, an invitation to raise our gaze to the ultimate horizon."[12]

Any artist will tell us that in making art there can be an analogy to the experience of spiritual transformation. When doing one's spiritual work or creating a piece of art, a certain abandonment of the self is important. Likewise, the artist offers herself to the creative impulse and worries not what is given the soul to reveal.

In the work of art, a canvas or piece of stone simply and blindly receives the stroke of the brush or the blow of the sculptor's chisel. It knows nothing of how the artist will shape it. It remains immovable in the hands of the artist, not asking what the creator will make of it. There is only an implicit and silent trust that the work will be the best possible and that it will reveal a beauty hitherto unseen or unknown. So the spirit of the artist must leave to the Creator what is prompted by the deeper Spirit and carry on peacefully with one's work. The artist and the work of art proceed together by a steady and simple submission, and a concentration on one's objective.

The work of the divine can never be anything but good and does not need to be reformed.[13] When the creative impulse is felt to be new and fresh, goodness and love become the transformative power of God's work within the artist. Like the spiritual life, making art can involve transforming a garbage dump into a sanctuary or, like a St. Francis, becoming a transhistorical, transreligious messenger of the love of life, of nature, and of the earth as sacred.[14]

As artists, we handle the notes like any other pianist. It's the pause—the contemplative pause—in between the notes where the art lies. The pause is where the Word of God finds root in our souls. When we are conscious of our possession of the Word, we will not be intimidated by any system of power. We take our power from the Word. Indeed, the Word of God is living and effective, sharper than any two-edged sword, penetrating even between soul and spirit and marrow, and enables one to discern reflections and thoughts of the heart. No creature is concealed from the Word, but everything is naked and exposed to the eyes of the One to whom we must render an account. We are called to be ministers of the Word.

## Healing

Several years ago and again in April 2010, Ronald Rolheiser, OMI, was asked to name the ten major spiritual questions in the Catholic world. Among them was the "struggle to live in torn, divided and highly polarized communities, as wounded persons ourselves, and [to] carry that tension without resentment, to be healers and peace-makers rather than simply responding in kind."[15] He emphasized that polarization will always be front and center, whether it's spoken or unspoken. Today the big ecclesial questions are about who has power and authority over sacraments, governance, and how the crisis of abuse is handled. Yet these are not the central questions about deep longings that reside inside and underneath the elemental human experience lurking through our worries and complaints. Under all this are our holy longings for healing and wholeness, an ache for the infinite, and a yearning for love.[16]

Deep wounds, long-standing grievances, senses of violation, and ruptures of trust give some idea of the terrain that roads to heal-ing must attempt to negotiate. Robert Schreiter, CPPS, outlines a threefold journey to reconciliation and healing. It is, first, about the human heart, not something we do, but what God is doing in us. Sec-ondly, it is about overcoming injustices, a central attribute of God without which the wounds of those who have suffered cannot heal. Thirdly, healing is about alternative social formations, where people come out of their own bounded zones to meet one another in a place that bears some of the marks of their home reality. These might be healing and listening circles, truth and reconciliation gatherings, or common-ground meetings for dialogue. It must be about change in all the parties involved—change as a matter of the mind, as well as of the body, which inscribes healing in the psyche of woundedness. A community of healing must be both a community of memory and a community of hope, for wrongdoing wreaks wounds upon the human heart and on the human community at the same time.[17]

Our healing powers are challenged by disease, by psychologi-cal and spiritual fragility. Again, the Gospel gives us all we need. There are more references to healing in the Gospel than any other activity of Jesus. Wondrous things come from a God who can do all things miraculously. We need transformative postures of expec-tancy, joy, possibility, intentionality, desire, and hope in God's goodness. We need healing and transformational images found in creation—sunrises, snowfalls, banquets of love, our companion travelers, personal and communal prayer, openness to graced power. These earthy and spiritual realities help us to truly know the capability of the human body to take on a characteristic that is consonant with what it believes.

Let us nurture the internal dynamic of the journey, allowing it to change us and to be affected by its unique nature, knowing that the arduousness, the discomfort of the journey, and the arrival are equally important. Taking our time seriously and elegantly, valuing our companions will assure us that we can "move forward securely, joyfully and swiftly," as Clare of Assisi wrote to Agnes of Prague.

No one should come into contact with us without receiving our mercy. This can happen only after we have done our own work of forgiveness. To be healed, to do penance, means to begin to consciously distance oneself from all that fragments our bondedness in human communion.

Reflect now on moments in which you have been stretched beyond your endurance, how you have been stigmatized, and how you have broken through it.

### Love

Ours is the only world religion whose one God became human. By virtue of God's immersion in the universe, the great waters of matter have been imbued with life and love. We are the recipients of this wild and universal love. We carry Christ in the enclosure of our souls. Bringing about a democratization of the incarnation is our mission because love is totally gratuitous; we are truth and love just by being created. T. S. Eliot wrote,

> Who then devised the torment? Love.
> Love is the unfamiliar Name
> Behind the hands that wove
> The intolerable shirt of flame,
> Which human power cannot remove.
> We only live, only suspire
> Consumed by either fire or fire.[18]

Religious life must be founded on a love relationship with Christ, first and foremost. If this is not the bedrock of our life form, nothing else will have efficacy—not community life, not social justice, nor any other effort at renewal or ministry that we take on. At the conclusion of the nineteenth assembly of bishops, dedicated to consecrated life, they wrote: "Throughout the history of the Church, Consecrated Life has been a living presence of the action of the Spirit, a privileged space of the absolute love for God and others, a witnessing of the divine plan to gather all of humanity within the civilization of love" (*Concluding Message*, October 27, 1994). Our sister Sandra Schneiders also notes that what the disciples share with Jesus as being God's children is the basis of both their union with him and their union with one another.[19] Ours is a spirituality of affectivity, that of becoming the One on whom we fix our gaze. Mutuality on either the human or divine level is not about equality; it is about dignity and the interdependency of mutual love.

Before he became pope, Cardinal Ratzinger said the church doesn't have "such an urgent need" for reformers, but rather what the Church really needs are "people who are inwardly seized by Christianity, who experience it as joy and hope, who have thus become lovers. Each vocation offers a particular answer to the questioning of genuine love, of loving what really matters."[20]

Writing to the Romans, Paul proclaimed: "And hope does not disappoint us, because God has poured out love into our hearts by the Holy Spirit, whom we have received" (Rom. 5:5).

## Conclusion

The mark of authentic Christianity has always been a paradox: it is thoroughly rooted in the earth, God's creation, and entirely bent on moving toward heaven, toward God. It is a dynamic balance. The virtue of hope is no different. Hope will give eagle's wings (Isa. 40:31) to our perseverance even as it restrains our flights of fancy. Hope is directed to God and God's beloved. It is focused not on external reality or hard facts but on God, God's justice, and God's faithfulness. Hope endures, not because life seems good or is the way we would have chosen it, but because we are committed to God.

We have been moving for over fifty years through massive renewal and reimagining of religious life. Some call it deconstruction. Now we are in the time of the "resurrection waltz" of reintegration.[21] The still point of the turning world is where the dance is.[22] We must shore up the foundations that make hope possible, live in hope and not just wait or look for it—"fierce faithfulness," this is called. The well of hope, a powerful urging in the depths of our souls, lies deep in each of us. As our beloved Mary Daniel Turner stated, "Intentionally and conscientiously we must now lay claim to our unique ecclesial identity: to be prophetic communities of hope who make Gospel imperatives a way of life, not rare expeditions into the Paschal journey, nor a private undertaking of individual sisters."[23] To focus on the person of Jesus while working for concrete reform in the functioning and organization of the church (Roman Curia, exercise of Petrine ministry, appointment of bishops, place of women, inculturation, authentic liturgy, realistic ecumenism) is a rightful role of ours.

Let us remember, however, that we will be known more by what we affirm than what we deny. Our whole being tends toward what we hope for. But we also know that the prophet, who is always concerned about a better future, is not known for nuance. Its two greatest enemies are conformity and comfort. Grounded in a sublime principle of the Second Vatican Council, we wait in stubborn hope[24] for truth to impose itself by virtue of its essence as it wins over the mind with both gentleness and power (*Dignitatis Humanae*, 1).

A young, trembling poet wrote:

Coiled to strike

My faith squirms
From grasping fangs
To soaring hopes

of escape . . .

I think not.[25]

Let us not doubt! Ours is a mission of love, healing, art, and prophecy. Embedded as we are in the present, we are creatures of the future. Our God is faithful and innovative. My sisters, my friends—let us be reverent stewards of these holy energies of prophecy, art, healing, and love. Let our charity give impetus to an unreasonable willingness to believe in and taste the future; to act together so that others might know and feel our love for the Gospel. And may the world find in us what it is looking for.[26]

How will we be reverent stewards of these holy energies of prophecy, art, healing, and love?

## Notes

1. J. Lora Dambroski, "In our own word . . . in our own time . . ." LCWR Presidential Address, New Orleans, August 14, 2009.

2. Fr. Nonomen, "A Holy Order: Where Would the Church Be without Women?" *Commonweal*, February 26, 2010, 8.

3. William J. Short, OFM, "Give an Account of the Hope That Is within You!" *Cord* 53, no. 5 (2003): 252, 254–55.

4. The schema for this presentation is found in Morton Kelsey, *Encounter with God* (Minneapolis: Bethany Fellowship, 1972).

5. These concepts are gleaned from Fr. Bruno Secondin, OCarm, in his May 2010 address to the UISG Plenary entitled "The Almond Branch and the Boiling Pot (Jer. 1, 11–13): What Is the Future for Our Mystical-Prophetic Heritage?"

6. Rabbi Arthur Green, "A Theology of Empathy," address given to UISG Plenary in May 2010, Rome, Italy. http://www.uisg.org/

7. Walter Brueggemann, "An Indispensable Upstream Word: The Gift of Prophecy," *Reflections: The Future of the Prophetic Voice* 93, no. 1 (Winter 2006): 49.

8. Henry James, "The Middle Years," *Scribners*, 1893.

9. Program notes to the recording of Olivier Messiaen, *Saint François d'Assise*, Salzburg, Felsenreitschule (August 1998), 21.

10. Anthony J. Gittins, CSSp, "Behold I Create a New Heaven and a New Earth, or, Hanging Baskets, Broken Strings, and a World Renewed," in *Mission Update* 19, no. 1 (Winter 2009): 6-11. The poetic references are from "The Darkling Thrush" by Thomas Hardy.

11. "Changing the Face of the Mountain," Franciscan Federation 2006. Adapted from a reflection by Linda Tan, OSF.

12. Benedict XVI, "Address to Artists, *Origins* 39, no. 28 (December 17, 2009): 454–57.

13. Jean-Pierre de Caussade, *Abandonment to the Divine Providence,* trans. John Beevers (New York: Doubleday, 1975), 81–83.

14. Frederick Franck, *Pacem in Terris: A Love Story* (New Paltz, NY: Codhill, 1979); and Marlene Weisenbeck FSPA, "Expressions of Beauty: A Tradition of Franciscan Art," Twentieth anniversary of the Franciscan Spirituality Center in La Crosse, WI, September 29, 2005.

15. John L. Allen Jr., "To Be Fully Human: Rolheiser Gets to the Essentials," *National Catholic Reporter,* May 28, 2010, 3a.

16. Donald Goergen, OP, *Fire of Love* (Mahwah, NJ: Paulist, 2006), 184–85.

17. Robert Schreiter, CPPS, "Reconciliation: Healing the Past or Building the Future," a paper delivered for "The Road to Reconciliation" Symposium at Boston College School of Theology and Ministry, April 16, 2009, and reprinted in *Mission Update* 18, no. 3.

18. T. S. Eliot, "Little Gidding," in "Four Quartets."

19. Sandra M. Schneiders, IHM, *Selling All: Commitment, Consecrated Celibacy, and Community in Catholic Religious Life* (Mahwah. NJ: Paulist, 2001), 292.

20. Carl Anderson. "Called to Love: Common Vocation, Uncommon Joy: Getting Beyond a Hope-Killing Culture, adapted from his speech from the CMSWR Congress in Washington, DC, September 11, 2009.

21. An observation made by a speaker at the Franciscan Federation Assembly of 2008.

22. This is an expression of the Reverend Bliss Williams Browne, one of the first women to enroll at Yale University and an Episcopal priest; quoted in *Reflections: The Future of the Prophetic Voice* 93, no. 1 (Winter 2006): 43.

23. Mary Daniel Turner, "Dying and Rising: Called to Be Prophets of Hope," in *Transformation* 19, no. 1 (Spring 2010): 1.

24. Mary C. Gordon, *Huffington Post,* April 6, 2010.

25. Ben Kruse, *Neighborhood News* (newspaper published by A Place of Grace Catholic Worker House) 13, no. 2 (Winter 2009): 4.

26. Katherine Feely, SND, "The Density of the Present," *Occasional Papers* 39, no. 1 (Winter 2010): 25.

# 10

## NAVIGATING THE SHIFTS

### *Pat Farrell, OSF*

— St. Louis, August 10, 2012 —

*In many ways, the presidential address of Pat Farrell represents for the LCWR both a culmination of what has gone before and a transition toward what is yet to come. It is an articulation of leadership at a time when the currents of the past seem to swell into a mighty, perhaps seismic, wave of change—a fundamental shift in sensibility and consciousness for women religious.*

*The focus of the world was on Israel and Gaza exchanging rocket fire; on a communal effort to rescue trapped miners in Chile; on a shooter invading a movie theater in Colorado; on an earthquake, tsunami, and nuclear disaster in Fukushima, Japan; and on participants in Occupy Wall Street taking over a small park in lower Manhattan in protest of the pursuits of American financial institutions.*

*The Vatican continued to struggle with financial scandals and leaks of private documents. The people of God began a celebration of the fiftieth anniversary of Vatican II; the apostolic visitation of women religious congregations in the United States concluded with a final report not made available to them. Nuns on the Bus traveled through nine states to highlight social justice concerns in the proposed federal budget, and two women religious defended Vatican critiques of their theological and ethical writings. The doctrinal assessment of the LCWR concluded that "serious doctrinal*

134

*problems" called for episcopal "guidance and approval, where necessary,"*
*of the LCWR's structure and work. With a steady gaze on both inner life*
*and wider world, Pat Farrell offered her sisters the tools to navigate the*
*change.*

—∭—

The address that I am about to give is not the one I had imagined. After the lovely contemplative tone of last summer's Assembly, I had anticipated simply articulating from our contemporary religious life reflections on some of the new things we sense that God has been doing. Well, indeed we have been sensing new things. The doctrinal assessment, however, is not what I had in mind!

Clearly, there has been a shift! Some larger movement in the church, in the world, has landed on the LCWR. We are in a time of crisis, and that is a very hopeful place to be. As our main speaker, Barbara Marx Hubbard, has indicated, crisis precedes transformation. It would seem that an ecclesial and even cosmic transformation is trying to break through. In the doctrinal assessment we've been given an opportunity to help move it. We weren't looking for this controversy. Yet I don't think that it is by accident that it found us. No, there is just too much synchronicity in events that have prepared us for it. The apostolic visitation galvanized the solidarity among us. Our contemplative group reflection has been ripening our spiritual depth. The fiftieth anniversary of Vatican II approaches. How significant for us who took it so to heart and have been so shaped by it! It makes us recognize with poignant clarity what a very different moment this is. I find my prayer these days often taking the form of lamentation. Yes, something has shifted! And now, here we are, in the eye of an ecclesial storm, with a spotlight shining on us and a microphone placed at our mouths. What invitation, what opportunity, what responsibility is ours in this? Our LCWR mission statement reminds us that our time is holy, our leadership is gift, and our challenges are blessings.

I think it would be a mistake to make too much of the doctrinal assessment. We cannot allow it to consume an inordinate amount of our time and energy or to distract us from our mission. It is not the first time that a form of religious life has collided with the institutional church. Nor will it be the last. We've seen an apostolic visitation, the Quinn Commission, a Vatican intervention of CLAR and of the Jesuits. Many of the foundresses and founders of our congregations struggled long for canonical approval of our institutes. Some were even silenced or excommunicated. A few of them, as in the cases of Mary Ward and Mary McKillop, were later canonized. There is an inherent existential tension between the complementary roles of hierarchy and religious that is not likely to change. In an ideal ecclesial world, the different roles are held in creative tension, with mutual respect and appreciation, in an environment of open dialogue, for the building up of the whole church. The doctrinal assessment suggests that we are not currently living in an ideal ecclesial world.

I also think it would be a mistake to make too little of the doctrinal assessment. The historical impact of this moment is clear to all of us. It is reflected in the care with which LCWR members have both responded and not responded, in an effort to speak with one voice. We have heard it in more private conversations with concerned priests and bishops. It is evident in the immense groundswell of support from our brother religious and from the laity. Clearly they share our concern at the intolerance of dissent even from those with informed consciences the continued curtailing of the role of women. Here are selections from one of the many letters I have received: "I am writing to you because I am watching at this pivotal moment in our planet's spiritual history. I believe that all the Catholic faithful must be enlisted in your efforts, and that this crisis be treated as the twenty-first century catalyst for open debate and a rush of fresh air through every stained glass window in the land." Yes, much is at stake. Through it all, we can only go forward with truthfulness and integrity. Hopefully we can do so in a way that contributes to the good of religious life everywhere and to the healing of the fractured church we so love. It is no simple thing. We walk a fine line. Gratefully, we walk it together.

In the context of Barbara Marx Hubbard's presentation, it is easy to see this LCWR moment as a microcosm of a world in flux. It is nested within the very large and comprehensive paradigm shift of our day. The cosmic breaking down and breaking through we are experiencing gives us a broader context. Many institutions, traditions, and structures seem to be withering. Why? I believe the philosophical underpinnings of the way we've organized reality no longer hold. The human family is not served by individualism, patriarchy, a scarcity mentality, or competition. The world is outgrowing the dualistic constructs of superior/inferior, win/lose, good/bad, and domination/submission. Breaking through in their place are equality, communion, collaboration, synchronicity, expansiveness, abundance, wholeness, mutuality, intuitive knowing, and love.

This shift, while painful, is good news! It heralds a hopeful future for our church and our world. As a natural part of evolutionary advance, it in no way negates or undervalues what went before. Nor is there reason to be fearful of the cataclysmic movements of change swirling around us. We only need to recognize the movement, step into the flow, and be carried by it. Indeed, all creation is groaning in one great act of giving birth. The Spirit of God still hovers over the chaos. This familiar poem of Christopher Fry captures it:

> The human heart can go the lengths of God.
> Dark and cold, we may be
> But this is no winter now.
> The frozen misery of centuries breaks, cracks, begins to move.
> The thunder is the thunder of the floes.
> The thaw, the flood, the upstart spring.
> Thank God our time is now.
> When wrong comes up to face us everywhere
> Never to leave us 'til we take
> The greatest stride of soul that people ever took
> Affairs are now soul size.
> The enterprise is exploration into God. . . .
> —Christopher Fry, "A Sleep of Prisoners"

I would like to suggest a few ways for us to navigate the large and small changes we are undergoing. God is calling to us from the future. I believe we are being readied for a fresh in-breaking of the Reign of God. What can prepare us for that? Perhaps there are answers within our own spiritual DNA. Tools that have served us through centuries of religious life are, I believe, still a compass to guide us now. Let us consider a few, one by one.

## How Can We Navigate the Shifts?
## Through Contemplation

How else can we go forward except from a place of deep prayer? Our vocations, our lives, begin and end in the desire for God. We have a lifetime of being lured into union with Divine Mystery. That Presence is our truest home. The path of contemplation we've been on together is our surest way into the darkness of God's leading. In situations of impasse, it is only prayerful spaciousness that allows what wants to emerge to manifest itself. We are at such an impasse now. Our collective wisdom needs to be gathered. It germinates in silence, as we saw during the six weeks following the issuing of the mandate from the Congregation for the Doctrine of the Faith. We wait for God to carve out a deeper knowing in us. With Jan Richardson we pray:

> You hollow us out, God, so that we may carry you, and you endlessly fill us only to be emptied again. Make smooth our inward spaces and sturdy, that we may hold you with less resistance and bear you with deeper grace.

Here is one image of contemplation: the prairie. The roots of prairie grass are extraordinarily deep. Prairie grass actually enriches the land. It produced the fertile soil of the Great Plains. The deep roots aerate the soil and decompose into rich, productive earth. Interestingly, a healthy prairie needs to be burned regularly. It needs the heat of the fire and the clearing away of the grass itself to bring the nutrients from the deep roots to the surface, supporting new growth. This burning reminds me of a similar image. There is a kind of eucalyptus tree in Australia whose seeds cannot germinate without a forest fire. The intense heat cracks open the seed and allows it to grow. Perhaps with us, too, there are deep parts of ourselves activated only when more shallow layers are stripped away. We are pruned and purified in the dark night. In both contemplation and conflict we are mulched into fertility. As the burning of the prairie draws energy from the roots upward and outward, contemplation draws us toward fruitful action. It is the seedbed of a prophetic life. Through it, God shapes and strengthens us for what is needed now.

## How Can We Navigate the Shifts?
## With a Prophetic Voice

The vocation of religious life is prophetic and charismatic by nature, offering an alternate lifestyle to that of the dominant culture. The call of Vatican II, which we so conscientiously heeded, urged us to respond to the signs of our times. For fifty years women religious in the United States have been trying to do so, to be a prophetic voice. There is no guarantee, however, that simply by virtue of our vocation we can be prophetic. Prophecy is both God's gift as well as the product of rigorous asceticism. Our rootedness in God needs to be deep enough and our read on reality clear enough for us to be a voice of conscience.

It is usually easy to recognize the prophetic voice when it is authentic. It has the freshness and freedom of the Gospel: open, and favoring the disenfranchised. The prophetic voice dares the truth. We can often hear in it a questioning of established power, and an uncovering of human pain and unmet need. It challenges structures that exclude some and benefit others. The prophetic voice urges action and a choice for change.

Considering again the large and small shifts of our time, what would a prophetic response to the doctrinal assessment look like? I think it would be humble, but not submissive; rooted in a solid sense of ourselves, but not self-righteous; truthful, but gentle and absolutely fearless. It would ask probing questions. Are we being invited to some appropriate pruning, and would we be open to it?

Is this doctrinal assessment process an expression of concern or an attempt to control? Concern is based in love and invites unity. Control through fear and intimidation would be an abuse of power. Does the institutional legitimacy of canonical recognition empower us to live prophetically? Does it allow us the freedom to question with informed consciences? Does it really welcome feedback in a church that claims to honor the *sensus fidelium*, the sense of the faithful? In the words of Bob Beck, "A social body without a mechanism for registering dissent is like a physical body that cannot feel pain. There is no way to get feedback that says that things are going wrong. Just as a social body that includes little more than dissent is as disruptive as a physical body that is in constant pain. Both need treatment."

When I think of the prophetic voice of the LCWR, specifically, I recall the statement on civil discourse from our 2011 Assembly. In the context of the doctrinal assessment, it speaks to me now in a whole new way. St. Augustine expressed what is needed for civil discourse with these words:

> Let us, on both sides, lay aside all arrogance. Let us not, on either side, claim that we have already discovered the truth. Let us seek it together as something which is known to neither of us. For then only may we seek it, lovingly and tranquilly, if there be no bold presumption that it is already discovered and possessed.

In a similar vein, what would a prophetic response to the larger paradigm shifts of our time look like? I hope it would include both openness and critical thinking, while also inspiring hope. We can claim the future we desire and act from it now. To do this takes the discipline of choosing where to focus our attention. If our brains, as neuroscience now suggests, take whatever we focus on as an invitation to make it happen, then the images and visions we live with matter a great deal. So we need to actively engage our imaginations in shaping visions of the future. Nothing we do is insignificant. Even a very small conscious choice of courage or of conscience can contribute to the transformation of the whole. It might be, for instance, the decision to put energy into that which seems most authentic to us, and withdraw energy and involvement from that which doesn't. This kind of intentionality is what Joanna Macy calls active hope. It is both creative and prophetic. In this difficult, transitional time, the future is in need of our imagination and our hopefulness. In the words of the French poet Rostand:

> It is at night that it is important to believe in the light; one must force the dawn to be born by believing in it.

## How Can We Navigate the Shifts?
## Through Solidarity with the Marginalized

We cannot live prophetically without proximity to those who are vulnerable and marginalized. First of all, that is where we belong. Our mission is to give ourselves away in love, particularly to those in greatest need. This is who we are as women religious. But also, the vantage point of marginal people is a privileged place of encounter with God, whose preference is always for the outcast. There is important wisdom to be gleaned from those on the margins. Vulnerable human beings put us more in touch with the truth of our limited and messy human condition, marked as it is by fragility, incompleteness, and inevitable struggle. The experience of God from that place is one of absolutely gratuitous mercy and empowering love. People on the margins who are less able and less invested in keeping up appearances, often have an uncanny ability to name things as they are. Standing with them can help situate us in the truth and keep us honest. We need to see what they see in order to be prophetic voices for our world and church, even as we struggle to balance our life on the periphery with fidelity to the center.

Collectively women religious have immense and varied experiences of ministry at the margins. Has it not been the privilege of our lives to stand with oppressed peoples? Have they not taught us what they have learned in order to survive: resiliency, creativity, solidarity, the energy of resistance, and joy? Those who live daily with loss can teach us how to grieve and how to let go. They also help us see when letting go is not enough. There are structures of injustice and exclusion that need to be unmasked and systematically removed. I offer this image of active dismantling that comes from Suchitoto, El Salvador, the day of celebration of the peace accords. That morning, people came out of their homes with sledge hammers and began to knock down the bunkers, to dismantle the machinery of war.

## How Can We Navigate the Shifts?
## Through Community

Religious have navigated many shifts over the years because we've done it together. We find such strength in each other! In the last fifty years since Vatican II our way of living community has shifted dramatically. It has not been easy and continues to evolve, within the particular U.S. challenge of creating community in an individualistic culture. Nonetheless, we have learned invaluable lessons.

We who are in positions of leadership are constantly challenged to honor a wide spectrum of opinions. We have learned a lot about creating community from diversity and about celebrating differences. We have come to trust divergent opinions as powerful pathways to greater clarity. Our commitment to community compels us to do that, as together we seek the common good.

We have effectively moved from a hierarchically structured lifestyle in our congregations to a more horizontal model. It is quite amazing, considering the rigidity from which we evolved. The participative structures and collaborative leadership models we have developed have been empowering, life-giving. These models may very well be the gift we now bring to the church and the world.

From an evolved experience of community, our understanding of obedience has also changed. This is of particular importance to us as we discern a response to the doctrinal assessment. How have we come to understand what free and responsible obedience means? A response of integrity to the mandate needs to come out of our own understanding of creative fidelity. Dominican Judy Schaefer has beautifully articulated theological underpinnings of what she calls "obedience in community" or "attentive discipleship." They reflect our post–Vatican II lived experience of communal discernment and decision making as a faithful form of obedience. She says: "Only when all participate actively in attentive listening can the community be assured that it has remained open and obedient to the fullness of God's call and grace in each particular moment in history." Isn't that what we have been doing at this Assembly? Community is another compass as we navigate our way forward. Our world has changed. I celebrate that with you through the poetic words of Alice Walker:

> The World Has Changed:
> It did not
> Change
> Without
> Your
> Numbers
> Your
> Fierce
> Love
> Of self
> &
> Cosmos
> It did not
> Change
> Without
>
> Your
> Strength.
>
> The world has
> Changed:
> Wake up!
> Give yourself
> The gift
> Of a new
> Day.

## How Can We Navigate the Shifts?
## Nonviolently

The breaking down and breaking through of massive paradigm shift is a violent sort of process. It invites the inner strength of a non-violent response. Jesus is our model in this. His radical inclusivity incited serious consequences. He was violently rejected as a threat to the established order. Yet he defined no one as enemy and loved those who persecuted him. Even in the apparent defeat of crucifix-ion, Jesus was no victim. He stood before Pilate declaring his power to lay down his life, not to have it taken from him.

What, then, does nonviolence look like for us? It is certainly not the passivity of the victim. It entails resisting rather than colluding with abusive power. It does mean, however, accepting suffering rather than passing it on. It refuses to shame, blame, threaten, or demon-ize. In fact, nonviolence requires that we befriend our own darkness and brokenness rather than projecting it onto another. This, in turn, connects us with our fundamental oneness with each other, even in conflict. Nonviolence is creative. It refuses to accept ultimatums and dead-end definitions without imaginative attempts to reframe them. When needed, I trust we will name and resist harmful behavior, with-out retaliation. We can absorb a certain degree of negativity without drama or fanfare, choosing not to escalate or lash out in return. My hope is that at least some measure of violence can stop with us.

Here I offer the image of a lightning rod. Lightning, the electri-cal charge generated by the clash of cold and warm air, is potentially destructive to whatever it strikes. A lightning rod draws the charge to itself, channels and grounds it, providing protection. A lightning rod doesn't hold on to the destructive energy but allows it to flow into the earth to be transformed.

## How Can We Navigate the Shifts?
## By Living in Joyful Hope

Joyful hope is the hallmark of genuine discipleship. We look forward to a future full of hope, in the face of all evidence to the contrary. Hope makes us attentive to signs of the inbreaking of the Reign of God. Jesus describes that coming reign in the parable of the mustard seed.

Let us consider for a moment what we know about mustard. Though it can also be cultivated, mustard is an invasive plant, essentially a weed. I offer the image of a variety of mustard that grows in the Midwest. Some exegetes tell us that when Jesus talks about the tiny mustard seed growing into a tree so large that the birds of the air come and build their nest in it, he is probably joking. To imagine birds building nests in the floppy little mustard plant is laughable. It is likely that Jesus' real meaning is something like, *Look, don't imagine that in following me you're going to look like some lofty tree. Don't expect to be Cedars of Lebanon or anything that looks like a large and respectable empire. But even the floppy little mustard plant can support life.* Mustard, more often than not, is a weed. Granted, it's a beautiful and medicinal weed. Mustard is flavorful and has wonderful healing properties. It can be harvested for healing, and its greatest value is in that. But mustard is usually a weed. It crops up anywhere, without permission. And most notably of all, it is uncontainable. It spreads prolifically and can take over whole fields of cultivated crops. You could even say that this little nuisance of a weed was illegal in the time of Jesus. There were laws about where to plant it in an effort to keep it under control.

Now, what does it say to us that Jesus uses this image to describe the Reign of God? Think about it. We can, indeed, live in joyful hope because there is no political or ecclesiastical herbicide that can wipe out the movement of God's Spirit. Our hope is in the absolutely uncontainable power of God. We who pledge our lives to a radical following of Jesus can expect to be seen as pesty weeds that need to be fenced in. If the weeds of God's Reign are stomped out in one place, they will crop up in another. I can hear, in that, the words of Archbishop Oscar Romero: "If I am killed, I will arise in the Salvadoran people."

And so we live in joyful hope, willing to be weeds one and all. We stand in the power of the dying and rising of Jesus. I hold forever in my heart an expression of that from the days of the dictatorship in

Chile: "*Pueden aplastar algunas flores, pero no pueden detener la primavera.*" "They can crush a few flowers but they can't hold back the springtime."

## Cited Sources

Beck, Robert. "Homily: Fifteenth Sunday in Ordinary Time," July 15, 2012. Mount St. Francis, Dubuque, Iowa.

Blastic, Michael W., OFMConv. "Contemplation and Compassion: A Franciscan Ministerial Spirituality." *Spirit and Life, Franciscan Leadership in Ministry* Vol. 7. St. Bonaventure, NY: Franciscan Institute, 1997, 147–77.

Cannato, Judy. *Field of Compassion: How the New Cosmology Is Transforming Spiritual Life*. Notre Dame, IN: Sorin, 2010.

Hubbard, Barbara Marx. *Conscious Evolution: Awakening the Power of Our Social Potential*. Novato, CA: New World Library, 1998.

Macy, Joanna, and Chris Johnstone. *Active Hope: How to Face the Mess We're in without Going Crazy*. Novato, CA: New World Library, 2012.

Richardson, Jan L. *Night Visions: Searching the Shadows of Advent and Christmas*. Orlando FL: Wanton Gospeller Press, 2010.

Schaefer, Judith K., OP. *The Evolution of a Vow: Obedience as Decision Making in Communion*. Piscataway, NJ: Transaction, 2009.

Silf, Margaret. *The Other Side of Chaos: Breaking through When Life Is Breaking Down*. Chicago: Loyola Press, 2011.

Walker, Alice. *Hard Times Require Furious Dancing*. Novato, CA: New World Library, 2010.

# EPILOGUE

In 1997, Katharine Graham printed her memoirs in a book entitled *Personal History*. A publisher by profession, Ms. Graham valued an economy of words. It is significant that she did not name it MY *Personal History*. That would have minimized its import, because the book was, in fact, the story of woman coming into her own in the twentieth century. While the circumstances were unique to Ms. Graham's lineage and talent, the dynamics reflect a much bigger story—the coming of age of women in the United States of America.

In a similar way, in *Spiritual Leadership for Challenging Times* we read an organizational history, the story of a women's institution coming of age in the world and in the Catholic Church in the late twentieth, early twenty-first centuries. The contribution of Catholic sisters to the building up of the United States is legendary, witnessed in the rise of schools and hospitals, tending soldiers on both sides of the conflict during wars, and feeding the hungry, often sacrificing their own meager stipends to provide for others.

This book complements that story by focusing on the inner life of an organization that brought the leaders of these women together, at the request of the Vatican, for education, interaction, prayer, and reflection so that their mission, their work toward furthering the Reign of God in the world could be more fully realized. This coming together began the slow and steady movement toward becoming ecclesial women as they heard one another into speech. This book illustrates the struggle of women trying to remain true to the Gospel and their founders' vision, simultaneously guided by the prophetic call in today's world and today's church. Illumined by the signs of the times read through the lens of the documents of Vatican II, these leaders listened to the new that was before them and within them— new insights, new images, new realities in an increasingly globalized world. Rather than departing from their essence, they remained radically faithful to their tradition, honoring both its institutional and prophetic dimensions.

Each of the addresses in this book stands alone and reflects the social, cultural, and ecclesial context of its time. Together they form a story of women maturing together and, in the process, developing a practice of leadership that recognizes, respects, and holds different perspectives. Believing in the wisdom of the whole, they listen to the minority voice among them, as well as that of the majority, and discern therein what truths in each contain direction for the common good.

In informal conversation, the theologian Monika Hellwig once said, "Religious life practices church for the church." She went on to explain that religious communities are small and nimble enough to stretch the limits of imagination, yet deeply rooted in the tradition which enables them to remain intact. Inherently part of the institutional church, these religious live at the edges of society and bring what they learn there to the center of the institution, even as they take the richness of the tradition to those at the edges of society who both hunger for and reveal a deeply spiritual center.

*Spiritual Leadership for Challenging Times* is the story of this rich dynamic—a body of women schooled in and motivated by a two-thousand-year-old religious tradition and eminently immersed in the twenty-first century. For many, they practice church for the church in a way that fosters communion rather than division. This is essential to the character of religious life. It does not splinter off and become a sect; rather, it offers a path of leadership and membership which models a way through in a pluralistic society.

The Leadership Conference of Women Religious is an organization that serves the elected leaders of more than three hundred institutes of Catholic sisters throughout the United States through opportunities for education, leadership training, consensus building, and action on matters that matter. This organization took seriously the call of the Second Vatican Council to encourage its members to update their own way of life and to become immersed in the joys and the hopes, the griefs and the anxieties of the people of God. Careful study of these conciliar documents and their own founding visions created a body of women who so love the world, that in imitation

of God, who became incarnate in the world through Jesus, they follow the Spirit's prompting to go anywhere and do anything for the
sake of the Gospel. In a way, they are the Catholic Church's first
responders. They go ahead to see needs that lie hidden; they assess
what must be done; they alert the church and society to emerging
needs, even as they immerse themselves in the new reality in order
to respond. In recent centuries, sisters did that in the United States
through the building of education, health care, and social service
systems to meet the needs of the volume of immigrants pouring into
this country. Today, while still providing direct service to current
needs, they attempt to raise the consciousness of those they edu-
cated and others who are now in positions of power to look at the
systemic causes of poverty, human trafficking, racism, and the plight
of current immigrants. What distinguishes them from a myriad of
social-service providers, however, is their quest for God. This is why
they exist. This hunger for God, this thirst for the way of God in our
world impels them to seek the face of God in everyone they meet.
This contemplative presence distinguishes their work; that they consistently do what they do with others, in communion with others,
marks how they do their work.

The LCWR's presidency, board, and staff assume leadership in
calling attention to current and emerging needs, by listening care-
fully to the experience of its own membership, and by trying to stay
abreast in our global society of what furthers the common good and
what is detrimental to society. It does this through disciplined prayer
and reflection, by careful listening and discernment, by experiment-
ing with directions and assessing their results. Attentive to the scrip-
tural maxim, "By their fruits you shall know them," this very human
organization is willing to make mistakes, acknowledge and learn
from them, and correct itself when necessary.

In recent years, the LCWR has become something of a lightning
rod during very complex times in the church and in the world. This
organization knows there are no easy resolutions to very complex
moral and ethical questions, and its attempt to take time to hear the
range of complexity is, at times, interpreted as disloyalty and even a

lack of orthodoxy. As a result, it has received support and condemnation from the public. Knowing there is always some truth in praise and in censure, the LCWR accepts both affirmation and criticism, and attempts to find the truth to which God calls it as an organization. Praise can strengthen and embolden; criticism clarifies and humbles. Both dynamics are important in the formation of leaders. Holding both in balance is a grace needed to go forward, individually and institutionally.

In this book, you experience the growing pains and moments of clarity within an organization of women growing together; you witness the maturing of an organization. Its leaders work together as one, while recognizing and urging the exercise of the individual gifts of each person as a gift to the organization. At this moment in the LCWR's history, it recognizes itself as a microcosm of women in the church and, in fact, of any organization that practices church for the church.

As you read this book, we invite you to reflect on your own contribution to the global common good. This endeavor, this seeking the common good in a globalized world for the sake of the planet itself and all its inhabitants will take the commitment of us all. The LCWR welcomes your partnership in this adventure and is exceedingly grateful for your companionship.

Janet Mock, CSJ,

Executive Director
Leadership Conference
of Women Religious
*June 2013*